PLANTS & GARDENS

BROOKLYN BOTANIC GARDEN RECORD

CULINARY
HERBS

1990

Brooklyn Botanic Garden

Printed at Science Press, Ephrata, Pennsylvania

Plants and Gardens, Brooklyn Botanic Garden Record (ISSN 0362-5850) is published quarterly at 1000 Washington Ave., Brooklyn, N.Y. 11225, by the ***Brooklyn Botanic Garden, Inc.*** Second-class-postage paid at Brooklyn, N.Y., and at additional mailing offices. Subscriptions included in Botanic Garden membership dues ($25.00 per year), which includes newsletters and announcements.

POSTMASTER: Send address changes to BROOKLYN BOTANIC GARDEN, Brooklyn, N.Y. 11225

ISBN #0-945322-06-9

PLANTS & GARDENS

BROOKLYN BOTANIC GARDEN RECORD

CULINARY HERBS

Revised Edition of Vol. 38, No. 2   Handbook #98

■

CONTENTS

LETTER FROM THE
BROOKLYN BOTANIC GARDEN

R ecipes in glossy magazines, and indeed in daily newspapers, make us aware that herbs are part of everyday cuisine as never before, in this country and many other parts of the world. In England Prince Philip's interest in herbs has given them the royal nod of approval — especially his enthusiasm for lovage, which is shared by both gardeners and cooks.

Gardeners are tending to use these plants freely instead of confining them to formal herb gardens. Parsley can be a frame for a flower bed; sweet woodruff an attractive ground cover;

chives an effective border. There are countless uses for thyme: One of the most inventive I remember was a mat of dwarf thyme at the center of a millstone made into an outdoor table on the Van Brunts' Westchester farm.

The late Elizabeth Van Brunt was Honorary Curator of Herbs for Brooklyn Botanic Garden from 1938 until her death in 1986. This was no sinecure: Apart from her editorship of BBG's Handbook on Herbs in 1958, and also of this Handbook on Culinary

The herb garden at the Planting Fields Arboretum, Long Island, seen through the draping branches of a quince tree.

4

Herbs, she was consultant for the Garden's film "Herbs: Use and Tradition," now a video. Much of the original was filmed in the Van Brunt living room and kitchen. One of the more colorful sequences was the making of a salad, garnished with bright nasturtium flowers, in a large wooden bowl. Elizabeth Van Brunt's students (she taught classes at BBG, both in Brooklyn and at the Kitchawan Research Center) will recall helping her with preparations for herb luncheons, for which the same salad bowl was used.

It was through Elizabeth Van Brunt's involvement with the New York unit of the Herb Society of America that this group developed an interest in BBG's Herb Garden, which celebrated its 50th anniversary in 1988, and which continues to be one of the most visited parts of the Garden.

We wish you, our readers, happy gardening and successful cooking with herbs.

Elizabeth Scholtz
Director Emeritus

Photo by Elvin McDonald

5

THE BASIC CULINARY GARDEN

MARY AND SCOTT PEDDIE

A small herb garden can be both a source of culinary delight and a thing of beauty. Even though most culinary herbs are not particularly attractive as individual plants, they can be combined, even in a small plot, to please the gardener's eye as well as his palate. My grandmother used to say, "Bread for my belly, but hyacinths for my soul." A well-designed herb garden will please both senses. In designing the garden one has a wide spectrum of colors, different foliage textures and distinctive growth patterns with which to work. Herbs which do add much appreciated color are chives, garlic chives, sage, oregano and borage.

Then there are the graceful members of the Parsley Family (Umbelliferae) such as anise, dill and fennel. None are vividly colored, but they are attractive in the garden, useful in fresh arrangements and, when dried, are stand-bys for more permanent displays. Chives (*Allium schoenoprasum*) deserve a place in every garden, their grasslike clumps producing ten to twenty mauve bell-shaped heads of flowers in spring. They are good for borders and as specimen plants in rock gardens. The white-flowered heads of garlic chives (*A. tuberosum*) do not

MARY AND SCOTT PEDDIE *are the proprietors of Rutland of Kentucky, specialists in growing herbs.*

dry as well as chives, but they have a unique beauty when they bloom in late summer. These are usually removed after flowering to prevent seeding, which can be a problem in a small garden. However, in larger areas it is often desirable to leave them, because the long-lasting scapes "swish-swish" in the autumn winds and become diamond-encrusted orbs in mid-winter.

Soil Improvement

Contrary to the oft repeated "Herbs do best in a poor soil," we find that they prefer a moderately rich, friable loam with good drainage and with more than the usual amounts of trace elements. However, helping a novice gardener acquire a "moderately rich, friable loam" is much like following the family recipe for spoonbread. "Half fill a bowl with cornmeal...a few eggs...and milk to the right consistency!" Amendments which improve the tilth of the soil include sand, perlite, peat moss, compost, gypsum (to loosen clay soils), well-rotted manure, peanut hulls—in fact anything that adds humus and improves soil structure. A good soil is to be cherished, and your herbs will appreciate it.

If you plan to grow herbs in containers, it is best to plant them in a "soilless" medium.

These are not the same as potting soils available in many stores. Garden centers or nurseries will have such mediums available. Some brand names are Metro-Mix, Sunshine Mix, Redi-Earth and Pro-Mix. These soilless mediums are light in weight and nearly sterile. Read the list of ingredients, and if a slow-release fertilizer (*e.g.*, Osmocote 14-14-14, three-month formulation) is not among them, incorporate it in the medium when you are ready to plant.

Perhaps the most satisfactory culinary herb garden is the raised bed, which ensures good drainage and is quick to warm up in spring, especially if it is in a sunny area, as it should be. A raised bed is also easier to tend than one at ground level because less stooping is involved. It can be made of brick, stone or cement block. Weathered railroad ties (not creosote-treated) are good, as are landscape timbers available at garden centers and lumber yards. Wood is easy to handle, comes in many sizes, and is aesthetically pleasing. If good garden soil is unavailable to fill in the area, there is a reasonable alternative. Raised beds are particularly nice if a soilless type of growing medium is used. The quickest method is to buy several bales of growing medium, but a less expensive method is to make your own. For a bed 6'x6'x12' the following combination of ingredients works well:

■

4 bags (5.5 cubic feet each) peat moss

2 bags (6 cubic feet each) perlite

2 bags (6 cubic feet each) vermiculite

1 bag (50 lb.) ground agricultural lime

1 bag (50 lb.) composted, dehydrated manure

10 cubic feet of sand

■

Spread two inches of sand over the bottom of the bed, then add the components in layers. Mix well with a spade, soak thoroughly and let the bed rest for 24 hours. Mix again, adding a balanced fertilizer, and level carefully. Sow seeds or set out plants and stand back! This herb garden will quickly produce an abundance of herbs with very little work.

What To Sow or Plant

Seeds versus plants is always a question. It is thrilling to sow seeds and then watch as the tiny plants appear. But unless you plan to make a great quantity of sausage, you are not going to need all sixty potential plants of sage that a packet may contain! Some herbs are best started from cuttings or root divisions, seed for others is virtually impossible to find, and true French tarragon can only be propagated vegetatively. Plan to buy some plants from a local nursery, or order them from one of the many mail-order herb specialists.

A basic culinary herb garden should have basil, chives, dill, garlic, lemon balm, marjoram, oregano, parsley, one of the mints, rosemary, sage, savory and a thyme or two. If the garden is for a serious cook, then tarragon must be added to the list.

Basil, dill, marjoram, oregano, sage and savory may be sown directly in the garden. Chives come easily from seed, but a well-established plant or two is advised. These will provide immediate cuttings for the kitchen, while the grasslike seedlings are becoming established. Parsley is very slow to germinate so purchasing a few plants locally in spring is advisable.

A mint is a must for every herb gardener, but certainly not in a raised bed. Mints are vigorous, invasive herbs and soon crowd out other plants. Plant them in a partially shaded area in soil which has enough humus to retain moisture well. An old-fashioned practice of planting mints near a water faucet was fine when water was piped out from the house. But now our faucets are located up against house walls, and the lime which leaches from the foundations of

A scarecrow stands guard over huge clumps of basil in this culinary garden.

newer dwellings, as well as the lack of sunlight and air circulation, causes many mints to languish. If only a small amount of mint is desired, plant it in a container sunk in the soil almost to the rim, so the roots will be confined.

"Rosemary is for remembrance"—and for tea and lamb and many other fine foods. Except in the milder parts of the country where it is winter hardy, it is grown as a tender perennial, thriving outdoors in summer and brought indoors in autumn to be overwintered as a house plant. Rosemary is beautiful, fragrant and useful; every garden should have one! It requires only careful neglect; that is, not too much water, time to grow, an open place with good drainage and gentle breezes. Container-grown rosemary plants need a thorough soaking at regular intervals. The prostrate variety is handsome as a cascade bonsai subject.

Here in Kentucky we find sage temperamental, in spite of its legendary long life. A number of problems, among them various diseases and root-destroying organisms, will suddenly attack a large plant. When grown is a raised bed in soilless medium, there is less chance of its demise. It is a wonderful gray-leaved, fragrant herb with many uses, but one well-established plant is enough for a basic culinary garden. Sage is quite ornamental in a perennial border.

Other Herbs

Both the annual summer savory and the perennial winter savory can be raised from seed. Summer savory grows and matures quickly, several sowings of a few seeds each providing cuttings for the kitchen all summer. The hardy winter savory is a durable plant, and a dwarf cultivar is nice in containers or where space is at a premium. All savories have the same sharp, peppery taste and go well with green beans. Two kinds of thyme seeds are generally available, winter thyme (*Thymus hyemalis*) and garden

8

thyme (*T. vulgaris*). The latter is easier to germinate and yields the larger crop, but winter thyme is an interesting subshrub with small gray leaves.

True French tarragon (*Artemisia dracunculus*) cannot be grown from seed. The tarragon seed which is often advertised produces a scraggly, weedy plant whose leaves have no flavor. True tarragon has such a distinctive and delightful taste that once you have begun to use it in the kitchen, you are an addict. Tarragon thrives in a moderately rich soil, but does require good drainage. It prefers full sun and yields best when well established. Tarragon plants should be divided every three or four years. Tarragon is excellent with chicken, in tartar sauce, and is a must in the *fines herbes* of French cuisine.

Unfortunately, a certain mystique has surrounded the growing of herbs. Some gardeners seem to think it requires special knowledge and labor to have an herb garden. Actually one need not have superpowers or a green thumb. They respond effusively to a moderate amount of tender loving care. If you do not have the space or time for a new herb garden, do begin by tucking plants into flower beds and vegetable plots, or in an unusual container. One word of warning, however, once you have begun to use fresh herbs in the kitchen, nothing else will do!

There are many other unusual and different culinary herbs to grow and use. Among them are anise and caraway for their seeds (if you can save them from the depredation of ants), and coriander, both for its fresh foliage for Spanish and South American dishes and the seed for candies and pastries. Then there is the bay (*Laurus nobilis*) of historical fact and fiction, a handsome house plant and valuable herb; also salad burnet, grown for its appealing whorl of leaves and cucumber flavor. Let your culinary herb garden reflect your artistic ability, your ethnic background and your talent as a cook!❀

Alliums and parsley add accent and texture to this handsome edible border.

Photo by Robert Kourik

9

HERBS IN THE SHADE

A.P. PATERSON

Herbs, we are usually told, are plants for the sun, and without it they languish and die. Why then offer a title of *Herbs in the Shade*? There are, perhaps, two main reasons why it is worth consideration. The first is that in any formally planned herb garden with beds in mirror image there are likely to be as many sites with a northern aspect as with a southern. The same plants do not necessarily succeed equally in each. Secondly, of course, herbs are often required to be grown in sunless gardens: the situation is not ideal and it would not be selected by choice, but if it is a question of that or no herbs, then better shade.

Categories and Conditions

The range of plants which can be considered to be herbs is very great. Two clear categories immediately suggest themselves: the medicinal and drug plants, such as foxglove and lily-of-the-valley, which produce potent and potentially poisonous glycosides and alkaloids; and culinary herbs with their aromatic essential oils. It is unfortunate for the requirements of shady-spot herb growing that while there are many plants in the first category which are natural woodlanders and hence prefer shade, there are virtually none in the second group that do not choose sun as long as adequate moisture is available. However, a third group of plants on the

A.P. PATERSON *is Director of Royal Botanical Gardens in Hamilton, Ontario, Canada and was formerly in charge of the Chelsea Physic Garden in London, England.*

fringe of herbal use offers plants which happily accept change. If, like sweet woodruff, they can be used as a tisane, or like primrose and violets, provide flowers for crystallizing, then they are legitimate candidates for a culinary herb garden.

The majority of perennial aromatic herbs ranging from large shrubby sages and rosemary to tiny thymes and savories are natives of the Mediterranean area. The climatic factors to which they are adapted are well known and indeed those very aromatic qualities are one of their adaptations, presumably for defense from browsing animals, though anyone who has seen the grazed-flat hillsides and tasted local roast lamb or kid will know it is not wholly successful!

Nonetheless, throughout hot rainless summers in thin alkaline soil they survive, making their annual growth in late winter or early spring when moisture is still available. Where shade exists in, for example, high evergreen thickets (maquis), most of the same herbs grow, but they are taller, more open (if less "typical") in habit. Shade is obviously not an inhibitor as long as there is excellent drainage and reasonable light concentration.

In cultivation similar criteria apply, but while plants may grow without certain seeming essentials, such a lack can make them more vulnerable in other ways, for instance, lessened hardiness. At the Chelsea Physic Garden in London we found that in the light sandy soil, supported by a remarkably winter-mild microclimate, Mediterranean aromatic herbs succeeded wonderfully under a canopy of deciduous trees and shrubs. Root competition for available moisture mattered much less than it would have with many plants.

Again, in all-shaded sites many of the conventional herbs will succeed if the building also causes a rain shadow effect so that soil never lies wet. Any possibility of slow drainage must be countered by the addition of humus or coarse sand or both. A bed raised above surrounding areas is always relished by these plants in any situation, sun or shade. If sunny sites are available, however, obviously they will be planted there. This leaves the shady areas for a further range of culinary herbs which may well succeed better there than in full sun.

Mints

The mints are the classic recommendation, and certainly they take shade well. Dry shade, however, is not enjoyed by them or others in this second group of shade-accepters (which is not at all the same as shade-lovers, a relatively small number of hardy plants including virtually no culinary herbs). What this group requires is adequate summer moisture at the roots as well as atmospheric humidity if their leafy tops—their usual culinary provision—are to be maintained in good condition for a long season.

It is not always realized what a wide diversity of visual effect and of fresh scent the mints possess when the leaves are crushed in the hand and when used in cooking. Scent and taste are such personal experiences, so evocative of individual memories, that to recommend is almost pointless. As many as

Mint

possible should be tried and one's own decisions made. The gray-leaved mints (based botanically on *Mentha villosa* and *M.* x *alopecuroides*) are useful visually, particularly when we remember that most gray-leaved plants need the sunniest spots. The vivid gold and green of ginger mint (*M.* x *gentilis* 'Variegata') and the white and green of pineapple mint (*M. suaveolens* 'Variegata') brighten dark corners. The purple-tinged bergamot or eau-de-cologne mint (*M.* x *piperita citrata*) provides a very different tone. It, to me, is the most delicious in the hand, quite wrong with peas or young lamb, yet good in the tiniest quantity with a salad or in an omelette *aux fines herbes*. The related bee balms (*Monarda*), especially those derived from *M. fistulosa*, will take similar conditions and provide floral height.

Parsley Relatives and Others

Several invaluable members of the Parsley Family (Umbelliferae) are happy with some shade. Parsley itself is also particularly keen on a moist atmosphere. Helped by shade, good leafy growth can be obtained from it throughout summer. It is almost impossible to have too much parsley, and several sowings should be made each year if one is really fond of it. Parsley also makes an admirable edging to beds. In spite of every statement to the contrary, I find the ornamental curled leaves just as tasty as the flat-leaved type.

Taller parsley relatives include fennel and angelica. The latter is one of the most ornamental of all herbs with its fine leaves and great green spheres of tiny white flowers. It is a biennial (though a freely self-sowing

11

one), hence it needs care to maintain the effect where it is wanted.

Fennel is rather like an angelica whose leaves have been scissored into the finest lace, making a cloud of green or of bronze-purple, depending on the form. Reasonable moisture in at least half-shade encourages foliage at the expense of the not very exciting flat plates of yellow flowers.

Other parsley relatives used herbally for leaves, such as dill, chervil (sown late summer for winter use in mild areas), celery and coriander do equally well in the shade. If, however, coriander is grown for its seed (and who wants ratatouille without it?), this herb must have sun. Sweet cicely, too, is highly effective as an ornamental plant and has an occasional flavoring role. Plants grow three or four feet tall, and the leaves often become unattractive by mid-summer. However, if the seeds are not required, the whole plant can be cut back sharply after flowering to encourage a bright green tuft of fernlike foliage for the rest of the season.

Both the common sorrel (*Rumex acetosa*) and French sorrel (*R. scutatus*) are happy in

Curly parsley makes an interesting edging for an herb garden or flower bed.

shade. The latter succeeds even in dry positions under trees. In such a spot it has to be replanted every so often, but this done, it provides good ground cover as well as succulent leaves for kitchen use.

Some of the onions, especially chives, are also shade-tolerant. Flowering may be reduced, but this is not important. Welsh or bunching onions, which are independent of floral fertilization for reproduction, are just as good. This is the basis upon which most herbs for shade can be selected. That factor taken into clear association with soil, the part of the country where you live, and the microclimate of your garden, should deal with most questions of "Will it or won't it grow?" Beyond this the answer is to try. Success frequently follows.❀

CONTAINER HERBS FOR WINDOWSILL OR TERRACE

LINDA YANG

An Elizabethan knot garden may indeed be a joy, but it's strictly a dream if you live in an apartment or small house where acreage doesn't exist. But don't despair. Fresh herbs for the table can be yours simply by growing them in pots or tubs on a windowsill, balcony, patio, terrace or rooftop.

The secret is to make the most of your limited space and take full advantage of whatever sun you may have. Most herbs will be satisfied with at least five hours of direct sunlight daily. They may never win a prize, but you can grow respectable rosemary, sage, thyme, chives, oregano, dill and coriander. If the growing area receives less than five hours each day but is not dark, you can still raise bay, parsley, tarragon, mint, basil, lemon balm and sweet cicely—and it's certainly worth experimenting with any others you enjoy.

Herbs can be grown in individual pots arranged on saucers on the floor or windowsill or in any other bright spot. Where space is

Gardeners with limited space can grow herbs in pots arranged on the floor or windowsill or outdoors on a terrace.

Photo by Elvin McDonald

13

minimal, by all means tuck several together into the same pot or into containers with other plants including vegetables, flowers and even shrubs and trees. Tub-sharing is standard procedure on many big-city terraces.

Any spare container will serve as a home for herbs, provided there is a hole in the bottom for drainage. Wooden tubs are especially practical since they don't break when moved about and won't crack if left outdoors during cold winters. Because non-hardy herbs such as rosemary and bay also make attractive house plants, in cold climates select pots for these which will also be decorative when the plants are taken indoors in autumn.

If there is insufficient rain during summer hot spells, watering, for small tubs in particular, may be a daily chore. Not only do containers retain less moisture than soil, but if terra cotta pots are used there is also evaporation from the sides. Plants in very sunny or windy locations may require watering twice daily, especially toward summer's end when they have filled their pots with roots. As the growing season progresses, you may well discover that the more herbs you cut and use, the more there will seem to be. That is the time to begin to dry or freeze some of the harvest in preparation for the lean days during the gray days of winter.❀

Preparation and Care

Once you've chosen a container, prepare it for the plants by lining the bottom with half an inch of pebbles or broken crockery. I like to cover this with a sheet of newspaper to keep the soil from dribbling out, and then add the potting mix. Most culinary herbs are not particular in their needs, but when growing in containers they fare better in a potting medium which drains well. One basic soil "recipe" useful for many herbs consists of equal proportions of topsoil, perlite, composted cow manure and peat moss along with a generous trowelful of bone meal for each 12-inch tub or average-size window-box. If you use a commercial potting mixture instead, add extra perlite to insure drainage. Fertilize container herbs every other week or so through the summer with a solution of fish emulsion diluted to half the strength recommended on the bottle.

LINDA YANG *writes regularly on city gardening for The New York Times. She is the author of* The Terrace Gardener's Handbook *and* The City Gardener's Handbook: From Balcony to Backyard.

ODE TO A VERY SPECIAL ALLIUM

Since things that here in order shall ensue,

Against all poysons have a secret power.

Peare, garlicke, reddish root, nuts, rape and rue–

But garlicke chiefe; for they that it devoure

May drinke, and care not who their drinke do brewe.

May walk in aires infected, every houre

Sith garlicke them hath power to save from death.

Bear with it though it makes unsavory breath.

And scorne not garlicke like to some that thinke

It only makes men winke, and drinke—and stinke!

*At the Medical School of Salermo, 1596.
A Rabelaisan verse written about garlic,
translated by Sir John Harrington*

HARVESTING HERBS

ELIZABETH B. NEAVILL

While herbs in a garden give aesthetic pleasure with their textures and subtle coloring, and are interesting for their lore and other associations, for many people the usefulness of these remarkable plants is their most important feature. When properly harvested, herb leaves, blossoms, roots and seeds can be used to enhance our diet, dye our fabrics, scent our belongings, decorate our homes and make our cosmetics. This article confines itself to the practical harvesting of culinary herbs.

Herb leaves can be harvested for immediate use, or they can be dried and stored for future needs. Among the so-called pot-herbs, whose young leaves are used fresh as a cooked vegetable or in soup, we find borage, chervil, chicory, sweet cicely, dandelion, good king Henry, lovage, white mustard, orach, rampion and sorrel. Fresh-picked herb leaves used in salads or as garnishes come from a wide variety of plants besides the common parsley—anise, lemon balm, basil, borage, burnet, caraway, chervil, chicory, chives, sweet cicely, dandelion, dill, fennel, lovage, marjoram, mint, white mustard, nasturtium, rampion, pineapple sage, savory, sorrel, French tarragon and sweet woodruff. Many of the salad herbs, plus other fresh herb leaves such as

horehound, oregano, rose geranium, rosemary and violet, plus violet blossoms and rose petals, can be used in the preparation of teas, jellies, meats, vegetables, desserts and candies.

How To Go About It

Drying herb leaves may not be as easy as snipping off fresh ones just before dinner, but its rewards are extremely satisfying. The task requires speed, care and simple equipment. The goal is to harvest the leaves when they contain the optimum amount of essential oils, that is, oils that volatilize at room temperatures and on which the flavor of the herb depends, and to retain during the drying process the color of the fresh leaves. To accomplish this, herbs ideally are cut soon after the dew has evaporated on a fair day which has been preceded by two full days of sunshine. They should also be cut when the flower buds are just beginning to open, except for mint, which has the most oil in its leaves when in full bloom.

Since the essential oils are volatile, as little time as possible should elapse between cutting and the start of the drying process. The herbs should be collected quickly but gently in an open-weave basket. Stacking them, or stuffing them into plastic bags, generates heat and causes rapid deterioration. If you must travel some distance after harvesting, transport the herbs with their stems in water, never cutting more

ELIZABETH B. NEAVILL *is an active member of the Western Reserve Unit of the Herb Society of America, which is responsible for the fine herb garden at the Garden Center of Greater Cleveland.*

Photos by Elvin McDonald

Herbs should be cut soon after the dew has evaporated on a fair day.

17

than can be conveniently dried at one time. A perennial herb may be cut back one- to two-thirds of its height, and an annual can be cut down to three or four inches. Get the harvest safely on the drying racks before taking time to shape the shorn plants for the additional growth that will produce a second harvest before September. The plants may be fertilized lightly with a nitrogenous fertilizer such as sulphate of ammonia to encourage the growth of new leaves.

Because time is literally of the essence in handling cut herbs, go through the washing process as quickly as you can. Cut away any undesirable material, and wash the herbs in warm water to remove all dirt or soil; never use cold or hot water. Three or four rinses are sometimes necessary. When they are clean, remove the herbs at once, then lay them on a bath towel and pat them gently dry. One innovative person I know lays the herbs lengthwise, not too many at a time, on a bath towel, folds each of its sides over the herbs, and picks up the towel at the ends to lay it around the drum in the basket of her automatic washer. She then spins the load one or two minutes and opens the washer to find the herbs, still neatly enclosed by the towel, ready for the drying rack!

Drying

A clean dark well-ventilated room with an evenly warm temperature ranging from 70-90 degrees F should be readied to house the herbs for drying. A dark air-conditioned room is ideal, and next best is an attic room whose windows may be closed at night. Racks with wood frames covered with muslin, cheesecloth or nylon net, or metal window screens with muslin or cheesecloth laid on top, should also be in readiness.

After they are washed, the leaves of basil, celery, dill, lemon balm, lemon-verbena, lovage, mint, parsley, sage and French tarragon are stripped by hand from their stems and placed in a single layer on each rack. Label each rack with the name of its herb to avoid confusion when dry. Racks should be elevated so air can circulate under and around them. Racks can be elevated from a table top by stacking books under two sides, or they can rest on the arms of chairs, or on the horizontal backs of two chairs. More professionally, they can slide into a frame especially constructed for them, with a space of at least one foot between racks.

Unlike the herbs with larger leaves, marjoram, oregano, rosemary, the savories and the thymes are dried first and then stripped. The stripping must be done with care and with clean dry fingers. One authority suggests wearing a glove on the stripping hand. For successful storing, be sure that all stems are removed when stripping small-leaved herbs.

Under normal circumstances herbs dry in three or four days, particularly if they are turned daily. In humid weather drying takes longer, and crisping is necessary as a final step. Herbs spread sparsely on a cookie sheet and placed in an oven at 125 degrees F will become crisp and ready for immediate storage in a few minutes.

Glass jars with screw tops will keep the dried herb leaves airtight until you wish to use them, summery-green and fragrant, on a cold and snowy day. Dried herb leaves are three times stronger than fresh ones, and this must be taken into account when they are used. When dried in the manner described, their flavor will be excellent for at least a year. Dried leaves stored whole retain their flavor longer than those stored rubbed, powdered or made into a mix with the blender.

Though chives can be dehydrated commercially by refrigeration, they do not dry satisfactorily in the home. However they, like parsley, can be frozen.

Herbs can also dry tied in small bunches and hung from cords strung in the drying room or attic. This method takes about a week. As soon as they are dry, they should be stored bunched, stripped or powdered in tightly covered jars. The results will be less satisfactory than with the screen method.

Blossoms and Roots

Fresh herb blossoms such as those of borage on a cake and nasturtiums in a salad, can be attractive as decorations. Chamomile flower heads, the yellow centers of which contain the essential oil, can be used fresh or dried for tea, and chive blossoms just starting to open make beautiful vinegar. The flower heads of calendula, snipped from their stems just before the last of them open, then dried well, are desirable fresh or dried in salads, soups and stews. Dried and stored in the same manner as herb leaves, herb blossoms are harvested in most cases at the moment when they have just come into full bloom. Fresh violets may also be candied at this time, and rose petals made into rose honey and rose syrup.

Herb roots for harvesting are dug in the spring or fall when the plant is inactive, at which time they are fullest of flavor and will not shrink. They should be scraped and hosed until clean, and if they are to be dried, the larger pieces sliced for uniformity of size and laid on the racks in the drying room for about six weeks. They should be turned over twice weekly and, if necessary, crisped in the oven, exactly as the herb leaves were, before going into airtight storage. A root is considered dry when it can be snapped smartly in two by the fingers. The roots of sweet flag, which are more tender in the spring, and of lovage can be candied fresh. Skirret root, to be boiled and eaten as a vegetable during the winter, may be stored in sand or left in the ground until needed. Roots of angelica, sweet cicely, elecampane and fennel are dried for candies, beverages and flavorings. The most widely used herb roots are the universal favorites, onions, garlic and shallots. A rope of braided dried onions hanging in the pantry at summer's end is a pleasant sight.

Seeds

The seed heads of anise, caraway, coriander, black cumin, dill, fennel, mustard and sesame are harvested when their stalks are dry and their seeds ripe. The heads, including a very short stem, are cut into a paper-lined basket, then spread in the drying room for five or six days, at which time the seeds can be loosened gently from their pods or stems. Remove the chaff and leave the seeds on the rack for another week or ten days, turning them often. Seeds, like all dried herb materials, are stored in airtight jars of a proper size in readiness for all kinds of culinary treats from soup to cake.✤

HERB OR ERB?

A simple four-letter word, h-e-r-b has been the cause of much discussion as to its pronunciation. In America one is often considered uncultured if he pronounces the h; in England he is apt to be branded a cockney if he drops the h.

Until 1475 the word was erb, both in spelling and in pronunciation. It came to England from the Latin herba, through the Old French herbe or erbe. At the beginning of the sixteenth century, the Latin h was re-attached to the word, but it remained mute until 1800. Since then pronunciation of the h has come into use; herb is correct in England. American usage still clings to the historical erb. Take your choice. When in London, say herb, when in New York say erb; when in Rome....

FAVORITES FROM

THE NATIONAL

ARBORETUM'S

HERB GARDEN

From the odd-shaped top onion to the long-bladed lemon grass

HOLLY HARMAR SHIMIZU

Using culinary herbs makes cooking a pleasure and puts challenge and creativity into the art of preparing food. Experimenting with different ones increases enthusiasm for cooking. The growing and using of herbs are not passing fads but practices that have been going on for centuries, ones that no doubt will increase as more information becomes available to the general public. The experience of the National Herb Garden at the U.S. National Arboretum in Washington, D.C., attests to this. Visitor interest there is very high, classes are always full and requests for information constant.

There are no strict limits to the use of herbs. However, until you are confident of how a certain herb is best used in cooking, it is suggested that you mix the herb, fresh or dried, with butter or cream cheese and sample it on bread. Once you are familiar with that flavor alone, finding interesting suitable combinations will come naturally. Although fresh herbs are not as concentrated as dry herbs, they are often preferred by cooks since the taste is better.

When I first started experimenting with herbs in the kitchen, I added so many different kinds that the food's natural flavor was completely disguised! I have since learned to be more subtle and use my herbs selectively. A general rule is not to mix two very strong herbs together, but rather to mix one strong and one or more milder flavors to complement the stronger herb along with, of course, the food. For this article I have selected ten of my favorites from the National Herb Garden. All are usually available as plants or seed, although some may have to be ordered from nurseries through the mail.

HOLLY HARMAR SHIMIZU *is Curator of the National Herb Garden at the U.S. National Arboretum in Washington, D.C.*

The National Arboretum's formal knot garden has corkscrew topiary accents.

Garlic and Top Onion

Garlic (*Allium sativum*) is foremost on my list. It is best known as a potent seasoning in French, Chinese and Italian cuisine. In salads, a clove may be rubbed simply in the salad bowl to give its flavor. In cooking, some people remove garlic from food before serving, others leave it. Garlic is commonly added to soups, sauces, dressings, meats, fish, pickles and curries. In addition, it is popular for flavoring butter, oil, vinegar and mayonnaise.

Requirements for growing garlic are full sun and rich, well-drained soil. Propagation is best by bulblets which should be planted in fall. New bulbs which have formed and are ready for harvest should be dried for one week and then may be trimmed, braided and hung in a cool, dry place.

A plant which always arouses comment in the National Herb Garden is the top onion (*Allium cepa* var. *viviparum*) because of its odd shape. On top of the 2- to 3-foot tubular scape (stem) a crown of small brown bulbils is formed. As the bulbils develop and get heavier, the scape falls to the ground, where bulbils begin to grow, thus forming new plants. The underground bulbs do not develop well; they are hardly thicker than the base of the stem. Despite their small size they are very flavorful and may be eaten in the same way as spring onions.

The bulbils of the top onion add onion flavor to hot dishes, to salads, and are especially good when pickled. One favorite treatment is to mix the bulbils in wine vinegar with white peppercorns, then heat for several minutes. Drain and set them into a jar, making layers with French tarragon and horseradish. Add the cooled vinegar over the layers and seal the jar. They make a delicious hors d'oeuvre.

Ocimum (basil)

Geranium, Perilla, Holy Basil

Many visitors are surprised to see the rose-scented geranium (Pelargonium graveolens) in the culinary herb garden. In my opinion its flavor and fragrance supersede the two hundred-plus other kinds of scented geraniums. Just a slight brush of the leaf and the delicious rose scent permeates the air. Originally from South Africa, this lovely plant is very easy to grow, its main requirements being full sun and good drainage. Keeping it cut back through the summer will give a full, compact plant. In order to hold it through the winter in areas with hard frost, plants should be dug in late fall and taken indoors for protection. Otherwise cuttings should be taken in late summer to grow for next year's garden.

Rose geranium leaves are used to flavor cakes and baked products. Whole leaves are placed on the bottom of the baking pan and then batter is added. During baking the flavor of the leaves will be absorbed by the cake and the leaves will leave their pattern on top of the cake. Another favorite culinary use of the rose geranium is to make jelly from leaves. It is made like other jellies except apple juice is added to yield a combination of apple and rose flavors. The chopped leaves are also added to sweeten fruit dishes and drinks, and even to make a delightful tea.

Also used as a tea are the leaves of purple perilla *(Perilla frutescens* 'Atropurpurea'). Although it is sometimes called weedy, purple perilla is a valuable garden plant both for its attractive dark purple foliage and its many culinary uses. Purple perilla is sometimes confused with 'Dark Opal' basil because of their similarity in foliage color. Actually, purple perilla is easy to recognize with its large, coarse leaves, which give it a much rougher texture than 'Dark Opal' basil, which has satiny smooth foliage. Purple perilla is a tender annual reaching a height of two to three feet. Although it self-sows prolifically, it is easily controlled by either cutting off the spikes of flowers as they fade or cultivating the surrounding soil in the succeeding spring to prevent seedling growth.

The uses of purple perilla are many. In Japan the leaves are an ingredient in mume (pickled Japanese plum) tea. They give dark red color to this tea, which is highly regarded as a medicine in that country and thought to be a cure against body parasites. The leaves are also dried and used as a flavoring in rice, adding a taste reminiscent of anise. Flowers are used to make an unusual tempura. Cut young flower spikes of purple perilla are dipped in tempura batter and deep fried. Young flowers tend to be less stringy and more flavorful. Flowers are added occasionally to soups as a seasoning. Also, young seedlings are used as a flavoring on raw fish.

An herb becoming increasingly popular is holy basil (*Ocimum sanctum*). In the United States it is often confused with spice basil, which *Tarragon* is actually a hybrid (possibly of *Ocimum canum* x *Ocimum basilicum*). In India, though, spice basil has been accepted as a holy basil because of its distinctive odor. True holy basil is also called *Sri tulsi* and *Krishnatulsi* in India. Holy basil is revered by Hindus and planted around temples. Cultivated in the warm regions of the Old World, it is a bushy perennial subshrub reaching a height of two feet. In cooler climates holy basil, like other basils, is grown as a tender annual. There is also a purple-leaved form of holy basil.

Holy basil's fragrance is similar to sweet cloves and is slightly intoxicating. Fresh leaves are added to salads for a sweet aniselike flavor. Fresh or dried leaves or even flower tops add tremendous taste to meats, especially chicken. Holy basil blends well with hot, spicy foods to give an almost cooling effect.

Chervil, Sweet Cicely, Lemon Grass

Imagine a piquant flavor somewhere between anise and tarragon. That describes the flavor of the leaves of chervil (*Anthriscus cerefolium*), which especially complements vegetable and egg dishes. It is an unusual garnish for pork, veal or beef. Chervil soup is quite delicious, as are chervil butter sauces. Chervil is very important in French cooking, being one of the traditional herbs used in the *fines herbes* mixture, which accounts for its synonymous common name, French parsley.

Chervil, which in fact resembles parsley in many ways, is a hardy, shade-loving annual that is not particular about soil. It is propagated by seed. Often grown in containers or window boxes, chervil can provide fresh leaves throughout the winter. Like most herbs it will fill out if cut back properly. The small white flowers, which form when plants are about eight weeks old, should be removed to encourage more leaf growth. If not cut back, the flowers are quickly succeeded by slender black seeds. Chervil grows best in spring or fall, tending to languish or die in hot, humid weather.

An herb with flavor similar to chervil but slightly sweeter is sweet cicely (*Myrrhis odorata*). Also referred to as sweet chervil, its anise flavor is so sweet that it may be used as a sugar substitute. Fresh leaves sweeten jams and tart fruit dishes. Finely chopped foliage enhances salads, salad dressings, vegetables (especially carrots), omelettes, pancakes and fish. The large taproots may be boiled and eaten with a vinaigrette sauce or candied. Commercially the seeds are used for their anise flavor in production of Chartreuse liqueur.

23

Not surprisingly its botanical name relates to its aniseed aroma, *Myrrhis* meaning perfume and *odorata* meaning fragrant. Along with great flavor and fragrance, sweet cicely is a most attractive herb, its young shoots appearing in early spring and uncurling into lovely ferny foliage. Soon white flower clusters appear from the center of the plant followed by shiny black seeds. Plants, which become large, need partial shade and an acid, moist soil. Propagation is by seed and by dividing the taproot into sections containing an eye. Sweet cicely requires a cool winter for its dormancy.

On the contrary, lemon grass (*Cymbopogon citratus*) likes the heat of the summer, thriving in hot tropical conditions. I am very selective about the tender herbs I will carry through the winter in the greenhouse, since space is limited, but lemon grass is one which deserves a place. Being a member of the Grass Family, the long-bladed clumps contrast with the textures of other herbs. The leaves, which grow from a bulbous base, are erect, to a height of roughly three feet, with a pleasant lemon scent. Lemon grass is unknown in the wild, although it is cultivated widely in the warmer regions of the world. Plants thrive in moist, ordinary garden soil with full sun and are easily propagated by division. It makes a good greenhouse or pot plant, benefiting from occasional use of a liquid fertilizer.

The leaves of lemon grass make a superb tea, often being used in combination with other tea blends. An essential oil is derived from the leaves and stems by steam distillation. This oil is important in cosmetic preparations, medicine and as a lemon flavoring. Since the oil is less expensive than other lemon oils, it is often used as a substitute.

Some Others

Many herbs, such as horseradish (*Armoracia rusticana*), are cultivated for their useful roots. Horseradish is best known for its use in hot sauce on roast beef and as an addition to catsup as a sauce for shrimp. As a garden plant it is best suited to the background, since it grows quite large, has a course texture and is invasive. Moreover, to harvest this plant the roots must be dug up. A vigorous, hardy perennial, its above and below ground parts reach lengths over three feet each. The roots, which emit a strong odor when bruised, can be eaten freshly grated as a condiment on may sorts of meats. They are dug in the fall, since that is when they contain the most flavor, and may be stored in cool, moist sand until needed. The roots may also be grated, mixed with a little vinegar and frozen. They are best used uncooked, as flavor is lost during heating. Grated into a sauce, the horseradish roots are added to salad dressings and fish. During summer young leaves make a fine salad green. In Gerard's *Herball* he wrote, "Horseradish stamped with a little vinegar put thereto, is commonly used among the Jermanes for sauce to eate fish with, and sauce-like meats as we do mustarde; but this kind of sauce doth heate the stomacke better, and causeth better digestion than mustarde."

Also cultivated for its roots and leaves is chicory or Belgian endive (*Cichorium intybus*). This plant is most likely already familiar to you since it thrives along roadsides, displaying its beautiful azure flowers in summer. It has been cultivated since Roman times as a vegetable and salad plant. Linnaeus referred to chicory as a floral clock because the blossoms open and close with the time of day.

Chicory is a hardy perennial preferring light, rich and well-drained soil. It is grown in different ways depending on how it will be used. Roots, when roasted, are a common substitute or adulterant for coffee, especially in France, while young green leaves are a desired salad green. Blanched young shoots are popular for salad. It is fairly simple to produce blanched heads of chicory. Dig the roots in the fall and plant vertically in deep boxes with soil, sand or similar medium between the roots. Then cover with pots, boxes or a light mulch to prevent light from getting in. Heads may be harvested in three to five weeks depending on temperature. Blanched leaves are extremely popular in Europe, the majority being cultivated in Belgium, hence the name Belgian endive.

The herbs discussed are a mere sampling of the rich palette of plants available to us. In planting a garden, even a landscape garden, I always feel combining beauty with usefulness gives double pleasure. Herbs then, particularly those with a culinary use, give infinite pleasure because their usefulness is unlimited. American nurserymen now report that sales of herbs are better than ever. Perhaps this is due in part to our new interest in good food, especially ethnic foods. Growing and using herbs adds new dimensions to our lives, not only through enhancing sweet and savory delights but through gardening, one of our most healthful hobbies. As Gerard wrote: "Talke of perfect happinesse or pleasure, and what place was so fit for that as the garden place where Adam was sent to be the Herbalist."🕸

Photo by Elvin McDonald

A potted myrtle topiary at the National Arboretum.

25

FAVORITES IN THE BBG HERB GARDEN

BERNARD CURRID

T he ten kitchen herbs I like the best? That's a difficult question because there are so many good ones, ones that give both garden worth and pleasure on the table. At the risk of inflating the list I will include a few aesthetically pleasing companion plants for the top ten! They also happen to be good kitchen herbs in their own right.

Basil 'Dark Opal', which has maroon foliage, is my first choice, a fine annual herb for seasoning and as an ornamental. Given sun and good drainage, which are the requirements of most herbs, it is an easy plant to grow, even as a winter foliage plant on the windowsill or under artificial lights. Young plants can be purchased in trays from garden centers in spring, or started indoors from seed six to eight weeks before they are set out in the garden once the danger of frost has passed. Frequent pinching of new shoots keeps plants compact and thrifty. Remove flower stalks as they form. Harvest leaves anytime, drying them or keeping them refrigerated.

BERNARD CURRID *has been in charge of the Herb Garden at Brooklyn Botanic Garden since 1968.*

A pleasing companion in the garden for basil 'Dark Opal'? I like to interplant it with salad burnet, which is a low-growing perennial herb with attractively cut foliage that has a light texture. Bear in mind that this purple basil is a handsome plant and holds up well in a flower border, especially when displayed with silver-leaved plants such as the dusty millers.

My second choice is caraway. I have a great affection for this herb of the Old Country. It is one of the first herbs I enjoyed as a child in my native northwestern Ireland. I remember tenderly, on special occasions, that the treat of the day was Irish soda bread to which was added a generous helping of caraway seeds and raisins.

Caraway, which has finely divided leaves much like a carrot, is a biennial which self-sows readily in the garden but not to the point of being a nuisance. The foliage is particularly attractive in early spring of the second year. Plants do not seem to thrive in summer heat or in very warm climates. Seedlings should be reset about a foot apart, with the excess weeded out. Older plants don't move well because they have tap roots.

When the umbels of seeds start to ripen they should be cut off and placed head down in a paper bag and left to dry in a warm, nonhumid place. Be sure to leave a few umbels to ripen on the plants to ensure selfsowing of seeds, which are winter hardy. There is another reason for leaving them. A few seeds are excellent to nibble on during a hot summer day when you are working in the garden and have a dry throat.

Chives, Bay and Thyme

Chives, which are perennial, are another favorite of mine. They have been cultivated at least since Charlemagne's time. With their purple blossoms in spring, chives are among the most attractive of all kitchen herbs. When the flowers fade I cut the plants back to the ground to encourage the growth of new leaves, which will eventually be snipped for use in salads or with sour cream for baked potato topping.

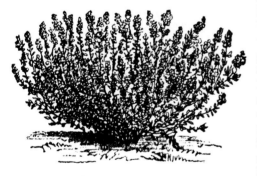

Thymus vulgaris (thyme)

There is a way to encourage even better flowering. In the Herb Garden at the Brooklyn Botanic Garden sometimes I have grown chives by planting single bulbs in spring, six inches apart and three inches deep, instead of transplanting small clumps, which is the usual method. The bulbs are kept well watered during summer. By the following spring there are healthy clumps with some very showy flowers. I therefore like to divide the chives bed in half, replanting a portion every other year.

Chives also grow well on a sunny windowsill or under lights. Grow several clumps and harvest one at a time, for this ensures a continued supply of soft fresh leaves.

Bay or true laurel (*Laurus nobilis*) is another herb of which I am very fond. In my own garden I grow this evergreen nonhardy shrub in the filtered light provided by fennel and dill plants. The bay is then brought into the house in autumn some three weeks before we turn on the heat. It thrives in a cool room with good light. In fact, bay makes an attractive house plant. Leaves are harvested fresh for kitchen use or dried, then stored in a jar. A hanging basket of curly-leaved parsley placed near the bay plant makes a nice winter accompaniment indoors, the finely cut light green foliage serving as contrast for the dark, somewhat heavy-textured appearance of the bay.

Thyme is my next choice, both in the BBG Herb Garden and at home, where I have a prostrate kind, mother-of-thyme (*Thymus serpyllum* of the trade), planted around the base of dwarf fruit trees. When the grass is mowed the combination gives an enchanting fragrance. Of course, we also grow thyme for kitchen use. Common

The knot garden, above, is the focal point of BBG's herb garden. Garlic chives, Allium tuberosum, right, put on an entrancing display in a corner of the garden.

29

or garden thyme (*T. vulgaris*) is the one my wife Fran uses the most.

Thyme needs sun and good drainage to perform well, and hardiness is not to be taken for granted in the North. If plants are grown in an open bed, some winter covering, such as salt hay or evergreen boughs, is advisable. On Long Island it is put down in December and removed in spring when crocuses start to bloom. At that time I prune out dead portions as well as the old woody stems, if there are any. At the Botanic Garden I have managed to save the dozen-or-so different varieties of thyme by this practice for over fourteen years.

Dried thyme leaves should be stored in airtight containers; or freeze the leaves as you would other herbs.

Rosemary, Sage and Others

Rosemary is a must for herb gardens as well as for remembrance. This tender narrow-leaved evergreen shrub has to be overwintered indoors in the North. Good drainage is essential, but plants should not be allowed to dry out; keep soil evenly moist. There are varieties with prostrate stems, attractive when grown over a wall or treated as a bonsai. I like to plant tarragon near rosemary for subtle contrast.

We are also fond of kitchen sage *(Salvia officinalis)*, a subshrub which grows about two feet tall. The soft gray-green leaves and violet-blue or white flowers, which are borne in summer, combine well with just about anything.

Sage is often a short-lived plant in the North, especially if drainage is poor, but the specimens at the Botanic Garden have stout woody stems and were obviously planted many years ago. There is a subtle point that might be mentioned in connection with the ornamental value of sage. The leaves are retained quite late into autumn and even into winter. They can be attractive after a snow, as can the gnarled branches.

Sage

Sage can be propagated by cuttings or from seeds. Plants should be spaced two to three feet apart. Be sure to remove spent flowers after bloom. Leaves can be harvested for kitchen use anytime during the growing season. Sage may be dried by hanging branches upside down in a warm dry place free from sunlight, so that the leaf color is retained.

Oregano and sweet marjoram, both of which are very useful herbs, are discussed in Gertrude Foster's article on page 28, so I will not mention them at length here. Oregano is reasonably perennial with us. Sweet marjoram, treated as an annual, is usually propagated by sowing seeds indoors in early spring six to eight weeks before setting out. This second step is performed after danger of frost has passed. Best leaf flavor is obtained just before flowering.

Mints

My favorite mints are peppermint, spearmint, pineapple mint and orange mint (the last also known variously as lemon, bergamot and eau-de-cologne mint). Most are indeed rampant growers, and at the Botanic Garden I confine them by setting out a few plants of any one kind in bottomless wooden boxes buried in the ground. The boxes protrude about one inch above the soil level. They are two feet wide and one foot deep.

Most mints perform best in filtered light. They also divide easily. Frequent pinching of stems produces bushy, compact plants. Sprigs may be dried in a dark, airy, warm room; or keep fresh leaves in plastic bags in the freezer.✿

A NOBLE JELLY

Holly Shimizu of the National Arboretum put horseradish on her list of ten favorite kitchen herbs (see page 16), and I heartily concur. There is no need to discuss its culture here, so I will close with a suggestion for a novel jelly which I first tasted during Old Home Day at Historic Richmondtown on Staten Island. Miss Margaret Robinson has been kind enough to supply the directions on how to make it. The ingredients consist of two cups sugar, one cup prepared horseradish drained, one cup white vinegar, red food coloring, one half bottle pectin. Boil sugar and vinegar three minutes. Add horseradish and return to a boil. Stir in coloring to tint desired. Stir in pectin. Bring to a full boil. Boil hard for one minute, stirring constantly. Remove from heat, skim and pour into hot sterilized jelly glasses. Seal with paraffin.

Makes three six-ounce glasses.

HERBS FOR TEA

Audrey H. O'Connor

Photo by Elvin McDonald

If you are cold, tea will warm you
if you are too heated, it will cool you
if you are depressed, it will cheer you
if you are excited, it will calm you.

— Gladstone

During the growing season, when your favorite culinary herbs benefit from pinching of flavorful tips and young leaves, get out your teapot with a thought for herbal teas or tisanes to cheer the colder months ahead.

The true mints yield their refreshing oils readily when two tablespoons of the fresh herb are infused in a pre-heated teapot (of china, glass or earthen-ware—never metal). The brewing method: pour a pint of freshly boiled water on the herb and steep for five to ten minutes. Then strain through a rush strainer directly into warmed teacups. Never boil herbal teas; do not add milk or sugar.

These tisanes can be invigorating or relaxing, to fit your mood or the time of day. Peppermint (*Mentha* x *piperita*) is the strongest flavor of the true mints. For variety try bergamot mint (*M.* x *piperita citrata*), apple mint (*M. suaveolens*), pineapple mint (*M. suaveolens* 'Variegata'), and the orange and ginger flavored cultivars. Experiment with other mint relatives from your garden when they are at the peak of their flavors: sweet marjoram, pineapple sage, the mountain-

Photo by Elvin McDonald

Chamomile: the plant, above, and the tea, left.

mints (*Pycnanthemum* spp.), anise-hyssop (*Agastache foeniculum*), lavender and rosemary. You may find a new flavor, as I did when leaves of Russian hyssop (*Hyssopus seravschanicus*) yielded a delightfully citric tisane, in contrast to the bitter flavor of *H. officinalis.*

Do lemon flavors grow in your garden? Lemon-verbena (*Aloysia triphylla*) is the most citric, tasting like lemon peel, but try lemon grass (*Cymbopogon citratus*), lemon thyme and lemon basil. Lemon balm (*Melissa officinalis*) supplies quantities of foliage, but it is relatively low in its essential oil; I find it loath to give much flavor, particularly when dried.

Once your favorite tea herbs are deter-mined, plan a harvest for winter supply. Follow the rules for gathering, drying and storing as for culinary herbs. To make tea from dried herbs, follow the brewing method for fresh herbs, but use one teaspoon of dried herb

AUDREY H. O'CONNOR *is the guiding light behind the outstanding Robison York State Herb Garden at the Cornell Plantations, Cornell University. She also served for many years as editor of* The Cornell Plantations *bulletin.*

for each cup. For cooling iced drinks, make a double strength brew of mint or lemon flavors, add ice and a slice of lemon or lime or a few borage flowers.

A different Kind of Tea Party

A tea-tasting party can be an adventure in the discovery of flavorful herbal blends. Ask your guests to bring their favorite tea plants to share experience about their culture. For those new to herbal teas, supply a tin of a mild green tea of pale color, to be modified with a choice of freshly dried herbal leaves for new flavors and dried flower petals for color. Violet, lavender, rosemary, borage, rose or calendula flowers or petals are decorative when floated in the cup.

Herbal tea enthusiasts should begin with a favorite herb flavor and blend with one or two milder flavors. An example would be chamomile (from dried flowers of the annual *Matricaria recutita*) as the base tea modified with apple mint and red clover. Or three mild flavors, such as elder flower, lemon thyme and bergamot, may be combined in equal strengths.

The blending of herbal flavors is an art. Care must be taken not to lose a subtle flavor by the addition of too much of a dominant flavor, such as peppermint or sage. If tempted to spice up a bland rose hip tea, add only a few cloves or bits of cinnamon stick. Ground spices become dust in the bottom of the blend and cloud the infusion.

Aroma, rather than color, is a guide to the tea's strength, since flowers and foliage vary in their yield of color. Some commercial blends include the calyx and bracts of the tropical roselle (*Hibiscus sabdariffa*) for color and acid flavor. This plant would be worth growing as an annual in southern herb gardens.

The tasting of blends is the criterion at your party. Individual tastes will differ; you will have as many favorite blends as you have guests. Each tea-taster should keep an accurate record of proportions used and should have the privilege of naming the blend.

From next year's garden I must test new flavors for teas; fresh angelica leaves, the flowers of chicory, the leaves of French sorrel and costmary. The decorative shiny black fruits of the star-anise (*Illicium verum*) deserve another trial. The anise flavor in an infusion has been elusive. I may have been storing the fruits too long, enjoying their beauty. I must remember to dry leaves of *Salvia dorisiana*. Will its flavor be as delightful as the fruit salad fragrance of its fresh leaves?

This joy of discovering new taste pleasures can be yours. Know your tea herbs by growing them in your garden, using them in your kitchen.❀

Here is a tea to be drunk on going to bed so one wakes neither sick nor sorry:

- One tablespoon lime blossoms (linden flowers, "tilleul," the most popular tisane in France)
- One tablespon rosemary
- One teaspoon sliced ginger root or one-half teaspoon powdered ginger

Warm pot; add two cups boiling water to ingredients. Steep fifteen to twenty minutes. Drink hot, sweetened with honey. Best results if drunk after one is in bed! (This was found by Elizabeth Remsen Van Brunt in an ancient family notebook.)

GATHER THE LEAVES SLOWLY

"Three-quarters speed ahead, but keep the anchor dragging" are the words of advice for those wishing to experiment with different plants for herbal teas. As candidates, stick to those plants you know from personal experience or have read about in Audrey O'Connor's article. There are, in fact, some toxic plants in just about any garden of size. This is nothing to be unduly concerned about, for it is unlikely that we will chomp on colchicum bulbs, mountain-laurel leaves or wisteria seeds. However, it is important to avoid brewing teas from plants whose properties we do not know. Even the sassafras tea that grandmother used to drink has been under suspicion lately as a carcinogen, and fatal accidents have occurred from people confusing foxglove (Digitalis purpurea), which is toxic, with comfrey (Symphytum officinale). There should be no hysteria, just knowledge, which will bring greater enjoyment of traditional herbal beverages.

And if you have a serious illness, go to a doctor. Do not rely on herbal teas to get you well.

— Frederick McGourty

THE ELUSIVE OREGANO

GERTRUDE B. FOSTER

When a four-year-old grandson sniffed a leaf of lemon balm, he wrinkled his nose and looked up knowingly. "That's the round yellow thing you put on fish," he said. Then more determinedly he added, "Why don't you plant these leaves and grow a lemon?" It's not a new idea that by planting one part of an herb you can change the character of the harvest! The herbalists suggested in 1539,

> "If you will have the leaves of the parcelye grow crisped, then before the sowing of them stuffe a tennis ball with the sedes and beat the same well against the ground whereby the sedes may be a little bruised or when the parcelye is well come up go over the bed with a weighty roller whereby it may so presse the leaves or else tread the same down under thy feet."
>
> *The Grete Herball*

Today gardeners sometimes are expected to transform sweet marjoram (*Origanum majorana*) into oregano by purchasing a plant and putting it in the garden. Oregano is a flavoring and scent which occurs in many different genera but is most often found in

GERTRUDE B. FOSTER *is the publisher of* The Herb Grower *with her husband Philip. She is the co-author of* Park's Success with Herbs *(Geo. W. Park Seed Co., Greenwood, South Carolina).*

the *Origanum* genus. The mixup within that variable genus may begin with the seed. Sweet marjoram seed may be labeled oregano, or vice versa. It is hard to blame the grower when John Parkinson stated in Chapter V of his *Theatrum Botanicum,* "There is much controversie among the Modern writers abut these two herbs." He was writing in 1640.

Straightening It Out

In 1947, the late Dr. George H.M. Lawrence, then director of the Bailey Hortorium at Cornell University, wrote for *The Herb Grower Magazine* a short piece on the distinction of the two species, *Origanum majorana* and *Origanum vulgare*, the latter of which was one source of the oregano flavor. Both were available as seed at that time through our Laurel Hill Herb Farm. Dr. Lawrence began by saying that "*Origanum* and *Majorana* are each good genera, but botanists and horticulturists have sometimes confused and muddled their identities by unfortunately placing species belonging to one or the other in juxtaposition; other botanists have treated them as belonging to a single genus.

"*Origanum* has the conventional more or less tubular calyx terminated by five teeth or lobes. In *Majorana* the calyx is split down one side and flares out, resembling a bract. See the drawing prepared by Marion Ruff, our staff artist, of the flowers of *Majorana hortensis* and of *Origanum vulgare* to better understand

Oreganos

this distinction of the calyx. There are other more superficial differences, notably that in *Majorana* the flowers are generally arranged in tightly congested globose to spike-like heads, whereas in *Origanum* they are more loosely disposed."

In *Hortus Third* the origanums are treated as a single genus again. This leaves it to the non-botanists to try to find the elusive oregano flavor among many, not just two, species. It occurs in *Origanum vulgare* in a variety known as *prismaticum*. The leaves closely resemble the type, also known as wild marjoram, and the flowers are on branching stems with overlapping bracts as well as five pointed calices.

The first oregano we grew in the early 1940s came from seed shaken out of a bundle of dried oregano marked "Product of Greece." The herb is cut while about to bloom or in full flower with some seed forming. It took a knowledge of small seeds to separate the chaff from the viable grains. The resulting plants were named *Origanum vulgare* var. *viride* by the Bailey Hortorium. At that time they did not have a herbarium specimen of *Origanum onites*, called pot marjoram. It, too, has the shell-like

formation of the calyx and is thus distinguished from wild marjoram. To separate it from sweet marjoram, now called *Origanum majorana*, Dr. Lawrence stated that there are 20-to-24-inch stems and unstalked or sessile leaves on *Origanum onites*, or pot marjoram. The leaves have reddish dotlike glands on calyx and corolla. These features must be observed with a magnifying glass. The scent of "Rigani," as pot marjoram is called on Crete, is brighter and sharper than either oregano or sweet marjoram.

For a time *Origanum onites* was in herb gardens in this country courtesy of Dr. and Mrs. Robert Whallon, who collected seed on the Island of Crete. *The Herb Grower Magazine* made available the handmade packets Mrs. Whallon sent from their own collection made in the wild. Unfortunately it did not prove hardy in many colder parts of the United States, and those given to nurserymen to propagate may not have seeded well or have become indistinguishable from other species of *Origanum* after they left the greenhouses.

Plants for sale in the spring are not usually in flower, so how can the gardener determine at that season which is sweet marjoram and which oregano? It is not easy unless you have felt, smelled and watched sweet marjoram produce its curious fat buds, which gave rise to the Elizabethan name of "knotted marjoram." They are composed of overlapping bracts which are rounded and split at the calyx to allow small white tubular flowers to protrude just a bit. The texture of the leaves is more velvety than those of *Origanum vulgare*, or oregano. The nurseryman won't appreciate having leaves pulled off plants to be felt and smelled. But you can lightly brush them and recognize the scent that you know from a jar of dried sweet marjoram. If there are blossoms, look for the above characteristics or the branching spikelets of pink or white flowers of *Origanum* species and varieties.

Others with Oregano Scent

To go back to our observer of similarities in aromas, the four-year-old, it may frustrate you to learn that there are several other genera of herbs with the same "oregano" scent and savor. One is *Coleus amboinicus*, native to tropical regions. Another is a species of *Monarda*, resembling *M. fistulosa*, sold as dried oregano in the southwestern United States and Mexico. The most readily available to herb gardeners in the North is a hardy, roundish-leaved species of thyme, one of several plants called Spanish thyme, *Thymus nummularius*. Its taste and smell are stronger than those of any member of the genus *Origanum*. The dried foliage is to be used as pizza flavoring with a lighter hand.

The genus *Origanum* also includes several other species grown for oregano flavor—*O. virens* (Spanish oregano), *O. sipyleum* from Turkey, and something called Greek oregano, which may be *O. heracleoticum* (less flavorful according to Dr. Whallon). All of which brings us back to the herbalists, particularly John Gerard, who in 1597 could say of marjoram, "it groweth in my garden," but he noted that some did not live over the winter in England. The best way to get acquainted with the herb is to grow it yourself, even if you have to shake seed out of a bundle of the dried imported herb.

Lucas Calpouso of Harvard University has stated in an article "Botanical Aspects of Oregano" in *Economic Botany* (Vol. 8, No. 3, 1954) that "the condiment name 'oregano' should be understood to refer not to any one species but to a particular spice flavor, furnished by plants of several genera in different parts of the world." To the herb gardener this is understandable, as costmary smells and tastes more like mint chewing gum than does spearmint, though it is in the Compositae, not in the Labiatae.✿

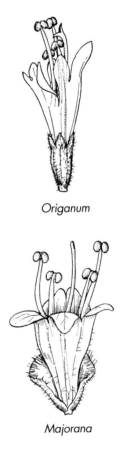

Origanum

Majorana

38

PROPAGATING CULINARY HERBS

HELEN WHITMAN

Propagating herbs for one's own garden is an excellent way to maintain and add to a collection, and also pays an extra dividend in interest and satisfaction—a feeling of having accomplished something worthwhile.

Most of the common herbs can be propagated easily by one or more of the usual methods of plant propagation—seeds, cuttings, division, or layering. Since these are standard horticultural techniques, they will not be discussed at length here. (For details of the various methods of propagation, see the BBG *Handbook on Propagation.*)

Growing from Seed

A great many herbs can be grown from seed with very little trouble. Annuals are best started out-of-doors in open ground after the soil has warmed up and danger of frost is over. In the vicinity of New York City this is about the first of May. The following annual herbs described in the dictionary section of this handbook, are easy to grow from seed:

anise	coriander
basil	dill
borage	fennel
calendula	nasturtium
caraway	summer savory

Some herbs are biennials, that is, they come from seed the first year but do not bloom and set their own seed until the following year. Most of these are also easy to grow from seed. Among them are burnet and clary sage.

With one or two exceptions, seeds of biennials are planted in spring like those of annuals. Angelica seeds are said to be very short-lived, so they should be sown as soon as they are ripe, in late summer. Parsley is also a biennial, but its flowers and seeds are of no particular interest to the herb gardener, so it is often treated as an annual. The seeds of parsley are very slow to germinate, taking as much as a month to six weeks, so they should be started in pots or flats in January for transplanting to the garden later. Soaking the seed in warm water for about 24 hours may hasten germination a little. Because parsley, like many other members of the carrot family, has a tap root, the seedlings are not easily transplanted except when very small. One way to get around this difficulty is to plant in small pots, two or three seeds in each. After the seedlings have started to grow, all but the strongest one in each pot are pulled out. When the plants are large enough to be planted in the garden, they can be turned out of the pots and put into the ground without injuring the roots.

HELEN WHITMAN *is an herb grower, garden designer and proprietor of Tool Shed Herb Nursery. She is also past chairman of the New York Unit of the Herb Society of America.*

Perennial herbs can also be grown quite easily from seed. They are best started indoors in flats in early spring and transplanted later to the garden. The following are frequently propagated in this way:

catnip	marjoram, sweet
cicely, sweet	marjoram, wild
horehound	pink, clove
hyssop	sage
lovage	savory, winter
marjoram, pot	thyme, common

Seeds of sweet cicely require exposure to cold for good germination and should be planted in fall to come up the following spring. If preferred, they may be stratified in moist sand or peat moss.

Division

Propagation by dividing the plants is practiced with a large number of perennial herbs, including the following:

Bees love the showy flowers of garlic chives (Allium tuberosum).

balm, lemon	mints
bible leaf	tarragon
chives	thyme, creeping
flag, sweet	thyme, lemon
horehound	violet, sweet
marjoram, pot	woodruff
marjoram, wild	

Divisions are best made in spring so the plants have plenty of time to become reestablished before cold weather.

Cuttings

Stem cuttings 1 to 3 inches long, taken from new growth and rooted in sand or vermiculite, provide a convenient way of multiplying many herbs. Among those often propagated in this way are:

geraniums, scented	rosemary
horehound	sage
laurel	sage, pineapple
lemon verbena	savory, winter
marjoram, sweet	thyme, common

Many of these can be taken at any time during the growing season, but in general spring is the best time.

Two herbs, woodruff and tarragon, are most frequently propagated by root cuttings rather than stem cuttings.

Layering

Layering is not such a common method of propagating herbs, but the thymes and no doubt several others, such as most mints, can be increased in this way.

GARDENS TO VISIT

Planning a kitchen border? See as many herb gardens as you can to get an idea of the plants in action, as well as inspiration for design. All of the places listed below have herb gardens within their larger frameworks. In addition, a number of restored villages and historic areas, too many to include here, have herb gardens well worth a visit.

Berkshire Garden Center, Rtes. 102 and 183, Stockbridge, MA 01262

Boerner Botanical Gardens, 5879 S. 92nd St., Whitnall Park, Hales Corners, WI 53130

Brooklyn Botanic Garden, 1000 Washington Ave., Brooklyn, NY 11225; outreach herb gardens are at BBG Research Center, 712 Kitchawan Rd. (Rte. 134), Ossining, NY 10562 and Clark Memorial Garden, 193 I.U. Willets Rd., Albertson, NY 11507.

Chicago Botanic Garden, Lake Cook Rd., Glencoe, IL 60022

The Cloisters, Fort Tryon Park, New York, NY 10040

Denver Botanic Gardens, 909 York St., Denver, CO 80206

Garden Center of Greater Cleveland, Western Reserve Herb Garden, 11030 East Blvd., Cleveland, OH 44106

Gardens of Cranbrook, 380 Lone Pine Rd., Bloomfield Hills, MI 48013

Hancock Shaker Village, Rte. 20, Hancock, MA

Longwood Gardens, Rte. 1, Kennett Square, PA 19348

Los Angeles State and County Arboretum, 301 N. Baldwin Ave., Arcadia, CA 91006

Missouri Botanical Garden, 2345 Tower Grove Ave., St. Louis, MO 63110

Montreal Botanical Garden, 4101 Sherbrooke St., E. Montreal, Quebec H1X 2B2, Canada

National Arboretum, 24th and R Sts. N.E., Washington, D.C. 20002

New York Botanical Garden, Bronx Park, Bronx, NY 10458

North Carolina Botanical Garden, Laurel Hill Rd., Chapel Hill, NC 27514

Old Sturbridge Village, Rte. 20, Sturbridge, MA 01566

Quincy Homestead, 1010 Hancock St., Quincy, MA

Strybing Arboretum, 9th Ave. and Lincoln Way, Golden Gate Park, San Francisco, CA 94122

Tennessee Botanical Gardens, Cheekwood, Cheek Rd., Nashville, TN 37205

Botanical Garden of the University of British Columbia, 1501 N.W. Marine Dr., Vancouver, B.C. V6T 1W5 Canada

Washington National Cathedral Bishop's Garden, Mt. St. Albans, Washington, D.C. 20016

Wave Hill Center for Environmental Studies, 675 W. 252nd St., Bronx, NY 10471

Wick Farm Garden, Tempe Wick Rd., Morristown National Historical Park, Morristown, NJ 07960

Robison York State Herb Garden, Cornell Plantations, Cornell University, 100 Judd Falls Rd., Ithaca, NY 14853

HOW TO KNOW F

T he great majority of herbs commonly grown belong to five large plant families: The mint, composite, parsley (or carrot), borage and mustard families. Each of these contains many members which differ from one another, yet all the members of any one family show certain "family resemblances" by which they can be easily recognized. The following brief descriptions and drawings point out the most important characteristics of those five families.

THE MINT FAMILY (*Labiate*) with square stems and mostly irregular, 2-lipped flowers having 4 stamens. The fruit is small, with 4 nutlets ('seeds'). Here we find: mint, basil, sage, ajuga, teucrium, rosemary, lavender, horehound, nepeta, agastache, lamium and thyme.

Flower cluster of thyme (left) and a typical flower of the Mint Family enlarged (right).

Flower head of a Composite (left), a disk flower enlarged (right, above) and a ray flower (right, below).

THE COMPOSITE FAMILY (*Compositae*), sunlovers with two kinds of flowers, ray and disk, combined into heads. Fruits are dry and hard, known botanically as achenes; they often have plumes of hairs to aid in wind dispersal. Here are elecampane, chicory, coltsfoot, chrysanthemum, tansy, artemisia, santolina, calendula and eupatorium.

THE PARSLEY FAMILY (*Umbelliferae*), often with hollow stems, flowers in flat-topped clusters called umbels. In this group fall: caraway, chervil, coriander, dill, fennel, cumin, lovage, pimpernel, myrrh, wild carrot, parsley, angelica, goutweed and skirret.

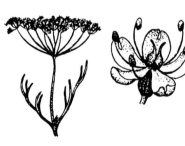

Umbel of flowers typical of the Parsley Family (left) with single flower enlarged (right).

Curved racyme of
flowers (left) typical of
the Borage Family;
single flower (right).

THE BORAGE FAMILY (*Boraginaceae*),
with tubular flowers mostly in curved
racymes and having 5 stamens
attached to the tube. The ovary is
superior, usually forming a fruit
composed of 4 nutlets. Among the
members of this family are: borage,
cynoglossum, forget-me-not,
mertensia, pulmonaria, symphytum,
anchusa, brunnera, echium and true
heliotrope.

THE MUSTARD FAMILY (*Cruciferae*), has
flowers with 4 petals forming a
square cross, 4 long stamens and 2
short ones, and superior ovary. Here
are: woad, mustard, peppergrass,
honesty, upland cress, dentaria, stock
and watercress.

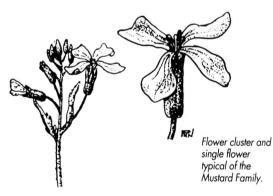

Flower cluster and
single flower
typical of the
Mustard Family.

ORNAMENTAL USES OF CULINARY HERBS

*h*erbs can be used for formal or informal effects. By utilizing the rich textures and subtle colors of herbs, patterns can be established and, with pruning, designs of various complexity can be maintained.

Photo by Christine M. Douglas

Photo by Elvin McDonald

44

Photo by Robert Kourik

Photo by Christine M. Douglas

Clockwise from top left:
BBG's herb garden features a central Elizabethan knot garden.
French tarragon's green feathery foliage contrasts with the purple leaves of Orach, Atriplex hortensis cultivar.
Close-up of the knot garden showing mulches of bark and white gravel.
Santolina in flower.

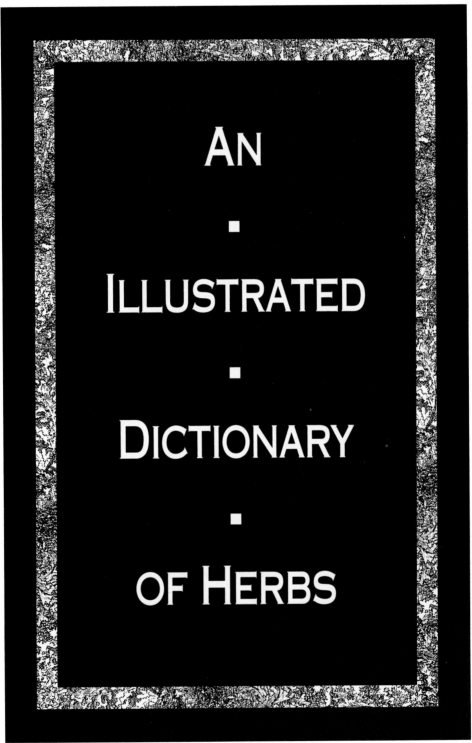

AN · ILLUSTRATED · DICTIONARY · OF HERBS

SWEET FLAG
(*Acorus calamus*)

A native plant having slender, lilylike leaves as long as 6 feet.

USE: Leaves and thick rootstalks have strong, aromatic, lemony odor and are used for sachets and flavoring. Roots can be candied. Also used in medicine.

HORTICULTURAL USE: Best grown in clumps and kept in background. Will grow in damp spots.

Culture: Thrives in wet soil and full sun, can be grown in drier places. Sweet flag is a hardy perennial, propagated by division.

Harvesting: Leaves can be used fresh; roots harvested in fall after plant dies down.

CHIVES
(*Allium schoenoprasum*)
(see page 48 for photo)

A small, dainty onion growing in clumps that reach about 10 inches high. Decorative light purple flowers in spring. Another species, garlic chives (*A. tuberosum*) has white flowers in late summer and may reach 3 feet in height.

Use: Leaves give a delicious onion flavor to foods.

Horticultural Use: Neat habit and attractive flowers make chives excellent as border plants.

Culture: Demands little care other than dividing on becoming over-crowded. Hardy perennials, chives are easily propagated by division or from seed.

Harvesting: The fresh leaves are cut for use as they grow.

GARLIC
(*Allium sativum*)
(see page 49 for photo)

Garlic is one of the flat-leaved onions, growing to about 2 feet. It has pinkish flowers in small heads.

Use: The bulbs, which break into small sections called "cloves," are a distinctive and well-known flavoring in many types of cookery.

Horticultural Use: The leaves and flowers are not unattractive, but the plant has no special horticultural value.

Culture: Grows in any good garden soil. Perennial, propagated by sets.

Harvesting: Mature bulbs dug and dried.

LEMON-VERBENA
(*Aloysia triphylla*)
(formerly *Lippia citriodora*)

A tender, woody shrub which in warm climates may reach 10 feet but is usually much smaller. In temperate climates it must be taken indoors in winter. The crisp, narrow, shiny leaves are strongly lemon-scented.

Use: The leaves are used for their fragrance and to give a lemony taste to teas, cold drinks, jellies, etc.

Horticultural Use: No special horticultural value; may be used as pot or tub specimens.

Culture: Will grow in any good garden or potting soil. Propagated from cuttings. Bring indoors at first signs of cold weather.

continued on page 50

Photo by Elvin McDonald

A. *Angelica, one of the stateliest of herbs, is usually treated as a biennial and grown from seed.*

B.*Chives (Allium schoenoprasum) have decorative light purple flowers in spring.*

C. *Garlic (Allium sativum) is one of the flat-leaved onions.*

Photo by Elvin McDonald

C

49

ANGELICA
(*Angelica archangelica*)
(see page 48 for photo)

A large, handsome plant which may reach 6 feet in height. The spreading leaves are divided into three-parted leaflets; the small greenish flowers are borne in rounded clusters (umbels) on the tops of the stems.

Use: Oil from the roots, leaves or seeds is used in perfumes; the leaves and stalks can be used as a vegetable. The principle use, however, is as a condiment or confection, the hollow stems being candied for the purpose.

Horticultural Use: Best for bold accent plant or as background for other plants.

Culture: Angelica is generally treated as a biennial and grown from seed. These should be planted in the fall, or stratified. Does best in a rather moist soil and cool climate.

Harvesting: Young stems are best for candying, roots and leaves are collected the second year of growth, seeds when ripe in late summer.

Angelica atropurpurea is native to the United States. It can be used in ways similar to *A. archangelica*.

DILL
(*Anethum graveolens*)
(see page 53 for photo)

Bluish-green stems contrast with finely divided, yellow-green, plumelike leaves and yellowish flowers. Grows to about 2 or 3 feet.

Use: Leaves and seeds famous for flavoring pickles, and also useful in other cookery, as with fish. Seeds yield a fragrant oil.

Horticultural Use: The finely divided light green leaves have a delicate, almost misty effect.

Culture: Dill is an annual that is easily grown from seed sown in spring after danger of frost. Should be sown in place, as it is not easy to transplant.

Harvesting: Leaves are best just as the flowers open. Seeds are picked when ripe.

CHERVIL
(*Anthriscus cerefolium*)

An annual growing 2 feet or less in height, with lacy leaves somewhat like parsley but lighter green. Flat heads of delicate white flowers.

Use: Chervil is used much as parsley is, in soups, salads, etc.

Horticultural Use: Requires semi-shade, so can be used in a shaded corner of the herb garden.

Culture: Raised from seed sown early in spring.

Harvesting: The fresh leaves are cut for use when large enough.

TARRAGON
(*Artemisia dracunculus*)
(see page 53 for photo)

Quite different in appearance and use from other artemisias, tarragon is an herbaceous perennial about 2 feet tall, much branched, with narrow somewhat twisted green leaves.

Use: The leaves of tarragon have a distinctive flavor a little like that of anise and are used in salads and other cookery. They yield their flavor to vinegar in which they are steeped.

Horticultural Use: No outstanding horticultural value.

Culture: Will grow in full sun, but seems to do better with a little shade. Propagated from root cuttings or by division. Protect in winter in cold climates.

Harvesting: Young leaves and stem tips are best to use fresh or to flavor vinegar. Flavor lost on drying.

BORAGE
(*Borago officinalis*)
(see page 56 for photo)

A decorative annual, with coarse, very hairy leaves and stems and beautiful sky-blue, starry flowers. It grows 2 to 3 feet tall.

Use: Flower sprays and leaves are used to impart a cool, cucumberlike flavor to summer drinks. It is said to be a good bee plant.

Horticultural Use: Valued chiefly for the beautiful color of the flowers. There are also white and reddish-purple varieties.

Culture: Easily grown from seed and will self-sow. Does best in dry sunny places.

Harvesting: The blossoms are picked as they open. The leaves are used fresh at any time; they are very seldom dried.

CALENDULA, POT MARIGOLD
(*Calendula officinalis*)
(see page 57 for photo)

A decorative annual, often grown in flower gardens. It grows from 1 to 2 feet tall, and has flat, round, many-rayed, yellow to orange flower heads.

Use: The petals of the flowers impart their yellow color and a subtle aromatic flavor to foods with which they are cooked. A tincture was formerly used in medicine.

Horticultural Use: Much prized for the brilliance of the blossoms.

Culture: Easily raised from seed after danger from frost is over. Will self-sow. Does best in bright sun.

Harvesting: The flowers are cut when fully open and the "petals" (actually florets) separated and dried in a shady place.

CARAWAY
(*Carum carvi*)

A biennial growing about 30 inches tall. The flowers are borne in flat white clusters and, like the finely cut leaves, resemble those of carrot.

Use: The seeds of caraway have a warm, aromatic odor and flavor and are popular in cooking. The oil is an important ingredient in liqueurs such as kummel.

Horticultural Use: Caraway has no special horticultural value, although the lacy leaves and flowers are rather attractive.

Culture: Easily raised from seed. Plants usually do not bear seed first year they are planted, but if started in fall will bear the following year.

Harvesting: Seeds picked when ripe.

BIBLE LEAF, COSTMARY
(*Chrysanthemum balsamita*)

Perennial that may grow to as much as 5 to 6 feet, with leaves 5 or 6 inches long and about 1 1/2 inches wide. They are light

continued on page 54

51

A. Chervil, an annual with lacy leaves, is used much like parsley in soups and salads.

B. The bluish-green stems of dill contrast with its finely divided, yellow-green, plumelike leaves and yellowish flowers.

C. Tarragon, a herbaceous perennial about two feet tall, has a distinctive flavor similar to that of anise.

A

Photo by Elvin McDonald

B

C

53

green, with small teeth on the margins and have a pleasant, camphory, mintlike fragrance. Flowers like small daisies.

Use: Leaves used for tea, and for their fragrance. They are also supposed to be useful as a moth preventive.

Horticultural Use: Best kept in the background as it grows large and is somewhat coarse.

Culture: Bible leaf is hardy and easily propagated by division. Does well in average soil, in dry sunny place.

Harvesting: Young leaves are cut before the plant flowers.

stigma. Beginners should not confuse it with the much larger colchicum which is also sometimes called autumn crocus and is poisonous.

Use: The orange stigmas when dried constitute saffron, widely used in cooking for its color and flavor.

Horticultural Use: Attractive as a welcome note of late color in the herb garden.

Culture: Grown from bulbs planted 4 inches deep in late summer. Need protection in the North.

Harvesting: Flowers picked as soon as open and stigmas removed and dried.

CORIANDER
(*Coriandrum sativum*)

A dainty annual growing to about 2 feet. The leaves are very finely divided, ill-smelling and tasting. Small white or purplish-tinged flowers in small flat heads.

Use: The globular seeds, about 1/8 inch in diameter, have a delicious perfumed taste and odor and are used as a condiment and in confections.

Horticultural Use: Attractive in clumps when in flower.

Culture: Easily grown from seed sown in spring. Does well in any good garden soil.

Harvesting: Seeds are picked when mature, before they fall.

SAFFRON CROCUS
(*Crocus sativus*)

A small, autumn-flowering crocus with lavender flowers having a bright orange

CLOVE PINK
(*Dianthus caryophyllus*)

Perennial, with jointed stems and blue-green, grasslike leaves and small carnation-like flowers. The fragrance of the flowers is penetrating and spicy, resembling cloves.

Use: Flowers are prized for their fragrance and used to flavor wine and vinegar.

Horticultural Use: Clove pink is a useful plant for a low border.

Culture: Can be propagated from seeds, cuttings, or by layering. It is hardy, but needs protection in cold climates. Should have good drainage.

SWEET FENNEL
(*Foeniculum officinalis*)
(see page 56 for photo)

This fennel is an annual growing to about 3 or 4 feet. The leaves are finely divided into threadlike segments, light green in color, or in one horticultural variety, maroon.

Use: The seeds are used as a condiment, the leaves for their aniselike flavor, and the stems can be eaten like celery.

Horticultural Use: No special value, but the leaves are attractive.

Culture: Grows easily from seed planted in spring.

Harvesting: Seeds are picked when ripe; the best stems for eating are the tender flower stalks, just before blossoming.

Other fennels: Florence fennel (*F. dulce*) is used as a vegetable, the thickened, bulbous leaf bases being cooked or eaten fresh. Bitter fennel (*F. vulgare*) is a perennial used much as the others are.

SWEET WOODRUFF
(*Galium odoratum*)
(see page 60 for photo)

Low spreading plant forming clumps about 8 inches high. The slender leaves are borne in starry whorls; the flowers are very small and white, in loose clusters. The plant, when crushed, and especially when dried, has a sweet scent of new-mown hay and vanilla. Formerly called *Asperula odorata*.

Use: The most famous use is for flavoring the German May-wine, and it can be used in other drinks.

Horticultural Use: Woodruff makes a charming ground cover under taller plants.

Culture: Can be grown as a perennial if winters are not too severe. In cold climates plants may be kept indoors or in cold frame over winter. Will thrive in half-shaded places.

Harvesting: Plants are harvested and dried in spring, when fragrance is strongest.

AMERICAN PENNYROYAL
(*Hedeoma pulegioides*)

A small, branching native annual that grows to about 18 inches. It has the mintlike odor of true pennyroyal.

Use: Used like true pennyroyal to make a tea for coughs and colds. Repels mosquitoes.

Horticultural Use: No particular horticultural value.

Culture: Does best in light shade. Grows from seed.

Harvesting: The whole plant is cut and dried just before flowering.

HYSSOP
(*Hyssopus officinalis*)

A hardy perennial growing to not more than about 2 feet, with woody stems, small pointed leaves, and spikes of small purple flowers. There are forms having pink or white flowers.

Use: The pungent leaves are used to flavor liqueurs and sometimes as a condiment. Oil obtained from them is used in perfumery.

Horticultural Use: Because it can be clipped, hyssop makes a good border plant or small hedge.

Culture: Will grow in rather poor soils and is easily propagated from seed. When established it is quite hardy.

continued on page 58

A. Fennel, shown here with the bronze leaves of Perilla, is a graceful, three-to four-foot annual whose seeds and leaves have an aniselike flavor.

B. Borage is a decorative annual with coarse, hairy leaves and a cucumberlike taste.

C. Calendula, or pot marigold, is often grown in flower gardens. Its flower petals impart their yellow color and a subtle aromatic flavor to foods.

LAUREL, BAY LEAF
(*Laurus nobilis*)

An evergreen tree which may reach 40 feet in height in its native Mediterranean region but is usually from 4 to 10 feet high and grown in containers in colder climates. It is the true laurel used for victory wreaths in classical Greek and Roman times.

Use: The glossy evergreen leaves are known to all cooks as bay leaves, used extensively in cooking.

Horticultural Use: Principally used as accent or specimen plants in tubs or boxes. Can be clipped.

Culture: Must be taken indoors in winter in any but semitropical climates. Requires rather rich, moist soil. Propagated from cuttings.

Harvesting: Mature leaves can be picked and dried for use at any time.

LOVAGE
(*Levisticvm officinale*)
(see page 60 for photo)

A hardy perennial herb with large, rich green leaves that resemble those of celery in appearance and taste, but stronger and sweeter.

Use: Leaves and stems give a celery flavor to soups and salads. Stem bases can be blanched and eaten.

Horticultural Use: Forms large clumps as much as 4 or 5 feet tall. Good background for smaller plants.

Culture: Does best in a rich, fairly moist soil. Propagated from seeds planted in late summer.

Harvesting: Leaves can be used fresh or dried at any time.

HOREHOUND
(*Marrubium vulgare*)

Somewhat coarse perennial, the entire plant covered with a whitish down. The leaves are crinkled and tend to turn downward.

Use: Horehound is the source of the familiar old-fashioned horehound candy.

Horticultural Use: The gray color of the plant provides a striking accent. Because of its weediness it is best kept toward the back of a planting.

Culture: Grows well in light soil, withstands full sun and intense heat. Hardy, but should be protected in very cold climates. Propagated from seed, cuttings, or by division.

LEMON BALM
(*Melissa officinalis*)

A somewhat weedy perennial growing to about 2 feet in height. The entire plant has a strong lemon scent.

Use: The leaves are sometimes used for tea, and sprigs are put into cool drinks to impart a lemony taste. Oil from the leaves is used in perfumes.

Horticultural Use: Lemon balm is best planted where it is not too conspicuous because of its weedy habit. It has a tendency to spread and must be kept within bounds.

Culture: Thrives in poor soil in a warm, sunny spot. Can be propagated from seed sown in spring, or by dividing.

Harvesting: Leaves and sprigs are picked in the morning whenever plants are large enough and used fresh or dried.

Peppermint
(*Mentha* x *piperita*)

Perennial with spreading rootstocks and numerous upright stems 2 feet or more tall. Dark green leaves and reddish-tinged stems have a characteristic warm spicy scent.

Use: Leaves used for tea and flavoring. Oil from the plant is used in confectionery and medicine and is the source of menthol.

Horticultural Use: No special value as an ornamental.

Culture: Does best in a rich, moist soil. Fairly hardy except where winters are severe. Propagated by division or cuttings.

Harvesting: Fresh leaves used at any time. Leaves to be dried are best taken just as flowering commences.

Pennyroyal
(*Mentha pulegium*)

Prostrate perennial with small oval leaves and creeping stems. It has a very pungent peppermintlike scent.

Use: Pennyroyal is used to make a tea for coughs and colds. The plant contains substances poisonous to some people so should be used with caution.

Horticultural Use: Could be used as a ground cover, but is somewhat weedy in appearance.

Culture: Easily propagated by division. Needs renewal every few years. It is a tender perennial which should be taken in over winter in cold climates.

Spearmint
(*Mentha spicata*)

Crisp-looking perennial with pointed, slightly crinkly leaves, lighter green than those of peppermint. The whole plant has a sweet characteristic odor.

Use: Leaves are used to flavor cold drinks, in teas, and to make mint sauce. Oil is used in confectionery.

Horticultural Use: No outstanding value, although its rich green color is pleasing.

Culture: Grows best in a somewhat moist soil. Propagated by cuttings or divisions. Hardy.

Harvesting: Fresh leaves and leafy stem tips picked any time. For drying, it is best cut just as flowering begins.

Note: Another species, apple mint (*M. suaveolens*), with rounded, hairy leaves, has become popular in recent years because of its strong flavor. One of the best in teas.

Bee Balm
(*Monarda didyma*)
(see page 61 for photo)

A handsome perennial that grows to about 4 feet, with beautiful scarlet flowers in round heads. The leaves have a pungent lemony scent resembling bergamot mint.

Use: Bee balm makes an aromatic tea.

Horticultural Use: The plants make strong clumps and the blossoms provide a welcome splash of color in the herb garden. There are varieties with deep red, violet, pink and white flowers. Wild bergamot (*M. fistulosa*) is very similar but has lavender flowers and there is also a white-flowered form.

continued on page 62

A. The most famous use of sweet woodruff (Galium odoratum) is for flavoring the German May wine.

B. The leaves and stems of lovage give a celerylike flavor to soups and salads.

C. Monarda, or bee balm, makes an aromatic tea. Pictured here is Monarda citriodora.

Photo by Elvin McDonald

Photo by Elvin McDonald

C

Photo by Elvin McDonald

Culture: Hardy and will grow in sun or light shade. Propagated by division or grown from seed.

SWEET CICELY
(*Myrrhis odorata*)

A very decorative perennial with downy, fernlike leaves and umbels of white flowers. It grows 3 to 4 feet tall.

Use: The green seeds have a spicy taste and are mixed with other herbs. They are used in certain liqueurs.

Horticultural Use: The delicate leaves and flowers are attractive and have a light airy appearance.

Culture: Grows best in partial shade. Seeds are planted in fall of the year or stratified.

Harvesting: Seeds are picked green and used fresh.

SWEET BASIL
(*Ocimum basilicum*)
(see page 64 for photo)

A pretty annual, about 18 inches tall, with light green rather broad leaves. The flowers are small and white, in spikes. There are several species of basil in cultivation, at least one having attractive purple leaves.

Use: The spicily-scented leaves are one of the most popular of all herbs used in cooking. They are considered especially good with tomato dishes, and are used fresh or dried.

Horticultural Use: The light green leaves are attractive, especially while the plants are young, and the purple-leaved kind, `Dark

Opal', gives an interesting color in the herb garden.

Culture: Grows easily from seed planted when danger of frost is over.

Harvesting: Leaves can be picked about six weeks after planting. For drying, it is best to cut them just before the flowers open.

SWEET MARJORAM
(*Origanum majorana*)
(see page 65 for photo)

One of the most fragrant and popular of all herbs. It is low and spreading, reaching about 8 to 12 inches in height, with small oval, gray-green leaves that are velvety to the touch. This species and the next were placed in the genus *Majorana* for many years.

Use: The fresh or, dried leaves are widely used as a flavoring in cooking. Oil is used in perfumery.

Horticultural Use: Gray-color foliage contrasts well with brighter greens. Can be used in borders.

Culture: Easily grown from seed or cuttings. In the North it is best treated as an annual or kept over winter as a pot plant. In the South it is perennial.

Harvesting: Use fresh at any time; cut leafy stems at flowering time and dry for future use.

POT MARJORAM
(*Origanum onites*)

Differs from sweet marjoram in being hardier and in having slightly larger leaves without stalks. The scent and flavor are somewhat more thymelike than those of sweet marjoram.

Use: Same as for sweet marjoram.

Horticultural Use: No particular horticultural value.

Culture: Grows best in a light limestone soil. Hardy in the vicinity of New York City, it should be taken indoors where winters are very severe. Propagated from seed or by division.

Harvesting: Same as for sweet marjoram.

WILD MARJORAM
(*Origanum vulgare*)

Hardy perennial with sprawling stems which may become 2 feet high. Much coarser than sweet marjoram, it smells more like thyme. Small pink or white flowers.

Use: The leaves are used as a flavoring in cooking but most people do not consider them as good as sweet marjoram leaves.

Horticultural Use: Weedy sprawling habit makes this plant of little value as an ornamental, but the flowers are pleasantly fragrant.

Culture: Grows well in poor soil, propagated by seeds or divisions.

ROSE GERANIUM
(*Pelargonium graveolens*)
(see page 64 for photo)

Tender perennial which must be wintered indoors in most of the United States. Where it can be grown outside the year around it may reach a height of 4 feet, but it is usually much smaller than this. The leaves are lobed and cut, rough to the touch, and smell of roses with an overtone of spice.

Use: The plants are grown commercially for the fragrant oil distilled from them. The leaves are used to give a rose flavor to desserts and jellies.

Horticultural Use: Rose geraniums are often used as pot plants, set in the garden in warm weather. The small lavender flowers are attractive but not showy.

Culture: Do well in any good garden soil, need sun. Propagated from cuttings.

Harvesting: The leaves can be cut at any time from mature plants.

PEPPERMINT GERANIUM
(*Pelargonium tomentosum*)
(see page 68 for photo)

This geranium has gray-green, velvety, shallowly-lobed leaves that smell strongly of peppermint.

Use: Peppermint geranium is used in potpourris and in cooking to give a peppermint flavor to jellies, desserts, etc.

Horticultural Use: Attractive bedding or pot plants.

Culture: Similar to that for rose geranium.

PARSLEY
(*Petroselinum crispum*)
(see page 68 for photo)

A hardy biennial usually treated as an annual. Grown for its much-divided, sometimes-curly leaves which have a characteristic odor and flavor.

Use: One of the most familiar of all herbs, used as flavoring and for garnish.

Horticultural Use: The beautiful green

continued on page 66

A. The leaves of rose geranium, a tender perennial which must be wintered indoors in most of the U.S., give a rose flavor to desserts and jellies.

B. Basil 'Spicy Globe' tastes similar to sweet basil but has a rounded, shrublike shape.

C. Sweet marjoram (Origanum majorana),one of the most fragrant and popular of all herbs, is widely used as a flavoring in cooking.

Photos by Elvin McDonald

leaves and compact habit of parsley in its first year of growth make it a good plant for edging.

Culture: Grown from seed started in early spring. Or purchase young plants then. Slow to germinate.

Harvesting: Cut any time when large enough. leaves are used fresh, or they may be dried in a slow oven (about 150 degrees F) until crisp.

ANISE
(*Pimpinella anisum*)

A dainty annual that grows from 1 1/2 to 2 feet high. It has lobed leaves, finely cut, and very small whitish flowers in flat clusters. The leaves and seeds have a warm sweet taste suggestive of licorice.

Use: The leaves are used in salads and as a garnish. The seeds are used to flavor confections, cakes, cookies, etc. Oil from the seed is used in medicine.

Horticultural Use: Attractive in the herb garden, but of no great ornamental value.

Culture: Grows readily from seed planted after danger of frost is past.

Harvesting: The green leaves can be cut whenever the plants are large enough. The seeds are gathered as soon as they ripen, dried and stored in tight containers.

BURNET
(*Poterium sanguisorba*)

A very pretty perennial with graceful compound leaves and oblong flower heads dotted with very small white or rosy flowers. It grows to about 1 foot high.

Use: The leaves have a cool flavor somewhat like that of cucumbers. They are used in salads and in cool drinks.

Horticulture Use: The graceful appearance and pleasant green of burnet leaves make it a useful plant near the front of a border, especially if the rather untidy flower heads are cut off.

Culture: Grows in any garden soil and is easily raised from seed. Burnet may also be propagated by division.

Harvesting: The fresh leaves are picked as wanted, and are best when young.

Rose
(*Rosa spp.*)
(see page 69 for photo)

Roses are not herbs, strictly speaking, but because of the beauty they bring to the herb garden, and because of the long use made of them in cooking and perfumery, they are usually included among the herbs. Those roses notable for their fragrance are the ones most appropriate for the herb garden, and among these the damask rose (*Rosa damascena*) is outstanding. Others are the French rose (*R. gallica*), cabbage rose (*R. centifolia*) and some rugose roses (*R. rugosa*).

Use: Petals are the source of attar of roses, and are used in potpourris, to make jams and jellies, and to give delicate flavor to various desserts. Hips are used for jam.

Horticultural Use and Culture: See *Handbook on Roses*.

Harvesting: Petals should be gathered on sunny day after dew is gone and when flowers are at height of bloom.

ROSEMARY
(*Rosmarinus officinalis*)
(see page 72 for photo)

Half-hardy perennial which is best taken indoors and kept as a pot plant over winter where climates are severe. Grows out-of-doors the year around in mild climates and may reach 3 to 6 feet. The narrow leaves are rather leathery, and have a spicy, resinous fragrance.

Use: A very popular flavoring for meats, dressings, etc. An oil from the leaves is used in medicine.

Horticultural Use: In warm climates rosemary can be used as a hedge. Makes a good specimen plant for growing in pot or tub.

Culture: Grows best in well-drained, sunny situation, in soil containing lime. Propagated by cuttings and can be grown from seed.

Harvesting: Fresh leaves cut at any time; for drying they are best taken just before plant blooms.

PINEAPPLE SAGE
(*Salvia elegans*)
(see page 73 for photo)

A tender perennial which must be wintered over in pots indoors in cold climates. The semi-woody stems may grow to over 4 feet high. The rough, pointed leaves have a delicious pineapple scent. Inch-long, tubular flowers of a beautiful cardinal-red appear in late summer. Formerly *S. rutilans*.

Use: The fragrant leaves are good in potpourris and give a pleasing flavor in cold drinks such as iced tea.

Horticultural Use: Because of its height and tendency to be scraggly, pineapple sage is best planted in the background.

Culture: Does well in any good garden soil. Propagated from cuttings, which will root in water.

Harvesting: Fresh leaves can be picked and dried at any time.

SAGE
(*Salvia officinalis*)

Woody hardy perennial with oblong, wooly, gray-green leaves, light below, darker above. Sage grows to 2 feet or more in height and has a tendency to sprawl.

Use: One of the most familiar of seasoning herbs, used with meats, dressings, etc.

Horticultural Use: If cut back from time to time sage is an attractive plant. There are dwarf forms useful for edging, as well as purple-leaved and variegated ones.

Culture: Does best in a light, well-drained soil in a sunny spot. Grows easily from seeds or cuttings.

Harvesting: Leafy tops of stalks are cut about 5 inches long before flowering, hung in open shade until dry.

continued on page 70

A. Peppermint geranium is used in potpourris and in cooking to give a peppermint flavor.

B. The beautiful green leaves and compact habit of parsley make it an attractive edging plant.

C. Rose petals are used in jams and jellies to give delicate flavor to various desserts. Rose hips are used for jam.

C

Clary Sage
(*Salvia sclarea*)
(see page 73 for photo)

This sage is a biennial, with large, pebbled, scalloped leaves as much as 9 inches long at the base of the plant, becoming smaller as they ascend the 3-foot flowering stalk. The flowers are whitish, in spikes with pinkish or lavender bracts. They have a strong aromatic odor.

Use: The leaves may be eaten in omelettes or fritters, and are sometimes used to flavor wines, ales and beer. Oil from the seeds is used in perfumes.

Horticultural Use: This handsome plant is decorative toward the back of a border.

Culture: Grows well in any garden soil. Grown from seed. After blooming the second year the plants are replaced.

Summer Savory
(*Satureja hortensis*)

A tender annual growing to 18 inches or less, with small, bronzy-green leaves and minute white or lavender flowers. The leaves are pungent and spicy.

Use: Summer savory is widely used as a condiment with meats and vegetables. It is generally considered a little sweeter-flavored than winter savory.

Horticultural Use: Not outstanding as an ornamental as the small leaves are sparse and less conspicuous than the stems.

Culture: Grows best in a well-worked loam. Seeds are planted out-of-doors in spring.

Harvesting: Leafy tops are cut when plants are in bud and hung in an airy shaded place until crisp and dry.

Winter Savory
(*Satureja montana*)
(see page 72 for photo)

This hardy perennial has dark green, shining, pointed leaves much stiffer in texture than those of summer savory. The plant is woody and grows up to 2 feet high. It has small white or lavender flowers.

Use: A very good condiment, not as sweet as summer savory. It is also used as a flavoring in some liqueurs.

Horticultural Use: Makes a good low hedge or accent plant.

Culture: Does best in a light sandy soil. Dead wood should be kept trimmed out. It is propagated by cuttings or raised from seed.

Harvesting: The young shoots and leaves may be picked at any time. The leaves are almost evergreen, but not so pungent in winter. They are best dried for winter use.

Common Thyme
(*Thymus vulgaris*)

Low growing, wiry-stemmed perennial reaching about 6 to 10 inches. The stems are stiff and woody, the leaves small, oval and gray-green. The lilac flowers are borne in small clusters. Leaves are highly aromatic.

Use: A widely used seasoning for food. Oil of thyme is used in medicine and perfumes. Famous as a source of honey.

Horticultural Use: Good as an edging plant or spreading among and over rocks.

Culture: Grows best in light, well-drained soil. It is well to renew the plants every few years. Propagated by cuttings, division and from seed.

Harvesting: Leafy tops and flower clusters cut and dried when first blossoms open.

MOTHER-OF-THYME
(*Thymus serpyllum* of the trade)
(see page 76 for photo)

Prostrate, spreading, shrubby perennial usually only a few inches in height. Small oval leaves and purple flowers. There are varieties with white, rose or crimson flowers, others with yellow- or white-variegated leaves. Lemon thyme (*T.* x *citriodorus*) has lemon-scented foliage.
Uses, Culture and Harvesting: Same as for common thyme.

NASTURTIUM
(*Tropaeolum majus*)
(see page 77 for photo)

Tender annual with juicy climbing stems and round, light green leaves. One of the most popular garden annuals because of its showy flowers in many shades of red, orange and yellow.
Use: The entire plant has a spicy, peppery flavor and the stems, young leaves and even flowers are used in salads. The green seed pods can be pickled as a substitute for capers.
Horticultural Use: Useful for trailing over rocks. Dwarf nasturtium (*T. minus*) is more useful as a border plant.
Culture: Grows in any good garden soil from seed planted after all danger of frost is over.
Harvesting: Fresh leaves and flower buds can be used at any time. The seed pods are used when full grown but still green.

SWEET VIOLET
(*Viola odorata*)
(see page 76 for photo)

Familiar hardy perennial with creeping root-stalks and heart-shaped leaves. There are over 600 kinds of violets known; this species is one of the most fragrant. Blossoms are deep violet and single.
Use: Grown chiefly for the beauty and fragrance of the blossoms. The flowers are occasionally candied and can be used in salads. The plant also is sometimes used medicinally. Perfume is obtained from the flowers, but much so-called "violet" scent comes from orris root.
Horticultural Use: Makes beautiful edging or border plantings. Also useful in partially shaded spots.
Culture: Thrives in poor soils especially in partial shade. Raised from seed or propagated by division.

A

B

Photo by Robert Kourik

Photo by Elvin McDonald

A. Satureja montana, winter savory, makes a good low hedge or accent plant.

B. Rosemary, a half-hardy perennial best moved indoors where winters are severe, is a popular flavoring for meats and dressings.

C. Pineapple sage, a tender perennial which must be wintered indoors in cold climates, gives a pleasant flavor to cold drinks such as iced tea.

D. The flowers of clary sage have a strong aromatic odor. Its leaves may be eaten in omelettes or fritters.

NURSERY SOURCES

Catnip Acres Herb Farm
67 Christian St.
Oxford, CT 06483
Seeds & plants; catalog $2

Cricket Hill Herb Farm Ltd.
Glen St.
Rowley, MA 01969
Plants

Fox Hill Farm
444 W. Michigan Ave., Box 9
Parma, MI 49269-0009
Plants & dried herbs

The Fragrant Path
P.O. Box 328
Fort Calhoun, NE 68023
Seeds; catalog $1

Gilbertie's Herb Gardens
65 Adams Rd.
Easton, CT 06612
Plants

Goodwin Creek Gardens
P.O. Box 83
Williams, OR 97544
Plants; catalog $1

Heirloom Gardens
P.O. Box 138
Guerneville, CA 95446
Seeds

Historical Roses
1657 West Jackson St.
Painesville, OH 44077
Roses; SASE

J.L. Hudson, Seedsman
P.O. Box 1058
Redwood City, CA 94064
Seeds; catalog $1

Logee's Greenhouses
141 North St.
Danielson, CT 06239
Plants; catalog $3

Nichols Garden Nursery
1190 North Pacific Highway
Albany, OR 97321
Seeds & Plants

Pickering Nurseries Inc.
670 Kingston Rd.
Pickering, Ontario, Canada L1V 1A6
Roses; catalog $2

Richters
Goodwood, Ontario, Canada LOC 1AO
Seeds & plants; catalog $4

Roses of Yesterday and Today
Brown's Valley Rd.
Watsonville, CA 95076
Roses; catalog $2

Sandy Mush Herb Nursery
Rte. 2, Surrett Cove Rd.
Leicester, NC 28748
Plants & seeds; catalog $4

Sunnybrook Farms
P.O. Box 6
9448 Mayfield Rd.
Chesterland, OH 44026
Plants

Taylor's Herb Gardens Inc.
1535 Lone Oak Rd.
Vista, CA 92084
Plants

W. Atlee Burpee Co.
300 Park Ave.
Warminster, PA 18974
Seeds

Well-Sweep Herb Farm
317 Mt. Bethel Rd.
Port Murray, NJ 07865
Plants; catalog $2

RECOMMENDED READING

BY DEBORAH KRUPECZK

The Complete Book of Herbs and Spices
by Sarah Garland
The Viking Press, 1979
An A-Z of herbs which includes description, cultivation and uses, as well as information on designing herb gardens, growing and harvesting and using herbs for cooking and seasonings.

The Harrowsmith Illustrated Book of Herbs
by Patrick Lima
Camden House, 1987
Divided into chapters including kitchen herbs, scented herbs and herbs used for teas. Contains cultural information and suggestions for incorporating herbs into the garden.

The Herb Garden Cookbook
by Linda Hutson
Texas Monthly Press, 1987
A cookbook with recipes primarily of Mexican and Southwestern flavor. Recipes for dishes from salads to fish, meat, drinks and bread with the 20 featured herbs. A brief description of the plant and propagation methods are given for each herb.

Herbs for the Home and Garden
By Shirley Reid
Angus and Robertson Publishers, 1987
An A-Z of herbs that touches on herbal lore, culture and propagation, as well as practical uses for cooking, with recipes utilizing each herb.

Herbs, Their Cultivation and Usage
by John and Rosemary Hemphill
Blanford Press, 1985
An A-Z of individual herbs with cultivation, culinary information and historical background for each. Includes a discussion of propagation methods and a section with interesting recipes.

Herbs, Their Culture and Uses
by Rosetta Clarkson
Collier Books
Macmillan Publishing Co., 1990
First printed in 1942; reprinted here with forward by Gertrude B. Foster. Many short chapters on ornamental uses, growing and recipes, and an A-Z at end with herb descriptions. Includes an appendix with tables on herbs for sun, shade, wet areas, etc.

Herbs Through the Seasons at Caprilands
by Adelma Grenier Simmons
Rodale Press, 1987
Divided into four sections: spring, summer, autumn, winter. Includes tips on growing herbs, from preparing the soil to mulching and harvesting. Choice recipes appropriate for each season. Includes a glossary of herbs with description, culture and use.

Kitchen Herb
The Art and Enjoyment of Growing Herbs and Cooking with Them
by Sal Gilbertie
Bantam Books, 1988
Guidelines for gardening with kitchen herbs. Includes practical and cultural information for 34 individual herbs, designs for theme herb gardens, using herbs in the kitchen and mouth watering recipes. Beautiful photographs illustrate each section.

Seeds
The Ultimate Guide to Growing Vegetables, Herbs and Flowers
by Sam Bittman
Bantam Books, 1989
Step-by-step information on growing plants from seed. Filled with practical tips on all aspects of planting and growing. Lists cultural information for 25 popular herbs. Beautiful color illustrations.

The World of Herbs and Spices
By James K. McNair
Ortho Book Series, 1978
Planting and culture of herbs. An A-Z of herbs and spices with descriptions and cultivation. A section of recipes and cooking ideas with a quick, illustrated guide to herbs and spices, giving common and latin names and uses for different plant parts.

A. Thymus serpyllum, mother-of-thyme, makes a good edging or plant between stepping stones.

B. Violets have lovely, sweet blossoms that can be candied.

C. Nasturiums add color and a peppery flavor to salads.

INDEX OF SCIENTIFIC NAMES OF PLANTS IN DICTIONARY OF HERBS

78

INDEX OF COMMON NAMES OF PLANTS IN DICTIONARY OF HERBS

Basil, olive oil and garlic combine to yield savory pesto.